About the Author

CHARLES ABBOTT is an intercultur
University of Westminster, London, a
Communications Training Institute a
language school with affiliates in four
he has worked as a consultant with Ita
and Naples. He has traveled extensivel
sales, and brings firsthand experience and professional insight to the
country and its people.

Other Books in the Series

- Culture Smart! Australia
- Culture Smart! Britain
- Culture Smart! China
- Culture Smart! Finland
- Culture Smart! France
- Culture Smart! Germany
- Culture Smart! Greece
- Culture Smart! Hong Kong
- Culture Smart! India
- Culture Smart! Ireland
- Culture Smart! Japan
- Culture Smart! Korea

- Culture Smart! Mexico
- Culture Smart! Netherlands•
- Culture Smart! Philippines
- Culture Smart! Poland
- Culture Smart! Russia
- Culture Smart! Singapore
- Culture Smart! Spain
- Culture Smart! Sweden
- Culture Smart! Switzerland
- Culture Smart! Thailand
- Culture Smart! USA

Other titles are in preparation. For more information,
contact: info@kuperard.co.uk

The publishers would like to thank **CultureShock!Consulting**
for its help in researching and developing the concept for this series.

CultureShock!Consulting

We are all likely at some time to be dealing with other cultures—foreign
visitors at home, e-mails from abroad, overseas sales agents, multicultural
teams within our organization, or a new foreign management structure.

CultureShock!Consulting creates tailor-made seminars and consultancy
programs to meet all types of corporate, public sector, and individual
intercultural needs. It provides pre- and post-assignment programs, as well
as ongoing "in-the-field" counseling worldwide.

For details, see www.cultureshockconsulting.com

contents

contents

Map of Italy

introduction

It is impossible to be bored in Italy. To excite, delight, and stimulate you there is the beauty of the land, the elegance and charm of its people, the variety of its regional cultures, the richness of its food and wine, the quality and dash of its design and engineering, the reputation of its artists, sculptors, writers, musicians, and filmmakers and, above all, the glory of its monuments and architecture. There is the sensuous pleasure of the Italian language, everyday as well as operatic; and the way Italians use diminutives and nicknames to create familiarity and intimacy with those around them. There is the whiff of intrigue and even scandal as well as tragedy in its history and politics, from the time of the ancient Romans, through the Renaissance right up to the present day.

Like all the *Culture Smart!* guides, this book focuses on the people. How do they behave, and what makes them tick? What is the best way to get on good terms with them? For that is the real way to enjoy Italy.

Above all other European nations, the Italians epitomize style. *Fare bella figura*—"to look good, to make the right impression"—is a social imperative, not a fashionable option. Some people have commented dryly that Italy represents a "triumph of style over substance." As this book shows, style is part of the substance—it helps explain the success of Italian design and fashion worldwide.

Like the other titles in this series, *CultureSmart! Italy* shows you as a foreigner how to get the best out of being in Italy and meeting and working with Italians. It tells you what you need to know about its history and culture and gives you a platform for further investigation of this fascinating country. It shows you how the Italians go about their daily lives, and highlights some of their passions and preoccupations. It introduces their festivals and traditions. It suggests how to have a good time in the Italian way, and gives tips on how to travel around. It offers a guide to communications, in particular to communicating successfully with Italians in a business situation.

Italian culture has been exported all over the world. What is it like at home? The Italians are the most European-minded of nations, emerging as they do from a long history of regional fragmentation, with some ancient battles still fought out on the football fields of Italy every week in season. This is your chance to get to know them better.

Key Facts

Official Name	Repubblica Italiana (Republic of Italy)	
Population	57.9 million (2001)	
Capital City	Rome (population 3.8 million)	
Other Main Cities	Milan (pop. 1.6 million); Turin (pop. 1,050,000); Genoa (pop. 706,000); Bologna (pop. 730,000); Florence (pop. 461,000); Venice (incl. mainland, pop. 274,580); Naples (pop. 1,050,000); Bari (pop. 450,000); Palermo (pop. 730,000); Catania (pop. 376,000).	
Area	116,310 sq. miles (301,245 sq. km)	
Climate	Mediterranean	
Currency	Euro (previously Italian lira)	
Ethnic Makeup	85% Italian national	
Language	Italian. Many distinct regional dialects.	German is spoken in Trento and Alto Adige. French is spoken in the Valle d'Aosta. Slovene is spoken in parts of Trieste and Gorizia.
Religion	No official religion	Roman Catholicism is the main religion
Government	Italy is a multiparty democracy with a president as head of state and a prime minister as head of government.	Elections are held every five years.

Media	Regional press with national distribution. Main newspapers: *Corriere della Sera* (Milan); *Il Messaggero* (Rome); *Repubblica* (Rome); *L'Osservatore Romano* (Vatican); *L'Unità* (Rome; formerly Communist, now more centrist); *La Stampa* (Turin).	Rai is the state broadcasting station with three TV channels (Rai 1, 2, and 3) and three radio channels (Radio 1, 2, and 3). There are also numerous commercial channels.
Media: English Language	The *International Herald Tribune* has an *Italy Daily* section covering Italian news. *Wanted in Rome* is an English-language news and listings magazine that comes out every two weeks. *L'Osservatore Romano* has a weekly English-language edition.	
Electricity	220 volts, 50 Hz AC, but check if older hotels still have 125 volts.	Standard continental plugs
Video/TV	PAL 625 lines	
Telephone	Italy's country code is 39.	Always put 0 before the local area code, even if dialing from within Italy (and even within the same town). To dial out, dial 00 plus country code
Time	One hour ahead of Greenwich Mean Time (G.M.T. + 1). Six hours ahead of U.S. Eastern Standard Time (E.S.T. + 6).	

chapter one

LAND & PEOPLE

GEOGRAPHY

Bordered on the north and west by Switzerland
and France, and to the northeast by Austria and
Slovenia, Italy's landmass extends south into the
Mediterranean, between the Ligurian and
Tyrrhenian seas in the west and the Adriatic and
Ionian seas in the east. Italy is first and foremost a
Mediterranean country and the Italians share
characteristics with other Latin nations—
spontaneity, and a relationship-based and not
particularly time-conscious society. Of the three
main islands off its coast, Sicily and Sardinia are
Italian, while Corsica—birthplace of Napoleon
Bonaparte—is French. The capital, Rome, lies
more or less in the center.

Italy is shaped like a boot, reaching down from
central southern Europe with its toe, Sicily, in the
Mediterranean and its heel, the town of Brindisi,
in the Ionian Sea. From top to toe it is about 1,000
miles (1,600 km) by the national expressway
(*autostrada*) network. The Brenner Pass in the
north is on the same latitude as Berne in

Switzerland, whereas the toe of southern Sicily is on the same latitude as Tripoli in Libya. Only a quarter of the country is arable lowland, watered by rivers such as the Po, Adige, Arno, and Tiber. The whole of the northern frontier region is fringed by the Alps, including the jagged peaks of the Dolomites, while the Apennine Mountains run like a backbone down the peninsula from the Gulf of Genoa to the Straits of Messina, with snow-covered peaks until early summer.

CLIMATE AND WEATHER

Italy's climate is Mediterranean, but northern Italy is on average four degrees cooler than the south because the country extends over ten degrees of latitude. The inhabitants of Milan, in the great northern plain of the River Po, endure winters as cold as Copenhagen in Denmark (40°F/5°C in January), whereas their summers are almost as hot as in Naples in the south (88°F/31°C in July)—but without the refreshing sea breezes. Turin, at the foot of the Alps, is even colder in winter (39°F/4°C in January) but has less torrid summers (75°F/24°C in July).

All the coastal areas are hot and dry in summer but subject also to violent thunderstorms, which can cause sudden flash floods. Inland cities such as Florence and Rome can be delightful early in the year (68°F/20°C in April), but unpleasantly heavy and sticky in July and August (88°F/31°C).

Spring and early summer and autumn are the best times to visit, though in Easter week Italian town centers are full of tourists, and in April and May they are packed with crowds of Italian schoolchildren on excursions. September and early October, when hotel rates and plane fares are cheaper, are often especially beautiful with clear fresh sunny days at the time of the grape harvest. October and November, the months of the olive harvest, have the heaviest rainfall of the year, but the winter months can also be wet, so take a waterproof coat and a good comfortable pair of walking shoes. (Naples has a higher average annual rainfall than London!) This is the time for the opera-goer, and the winter sports enthusiast, or to enjoy crowd-free shopping in Milan, Rome, or Venice. But before February is out, the pink almond is already blossoming in the South.

POPULATION

Italy's population is about 58 million, but the country has the second-lowest birth rate in Europe (after Spain). It has been estimated that the population could fall to 52 million within fifty years.

One reason for this is smaller families as more and more women seek their own careers, even though women still make up only a relatively small percentage of the professional and technical workforce. While 88 percent of all Italian women have one child, over half decide not to have another. Interestingly, the life expectancy of Italian women has doubled in fifty years to an average age of eighty-two.

According to UN estimates, some 300,000 immigrant workers a year will be needed to maintain Italy's workforce. There has been a steady stream of migrants from North Africa and the Far East, but the majority now come from central and southeastern Europe. Although Italy has made some attempts to curb immigration, these foreign workers are also regarded as "useful invaders." For decades, Italy was a land of emigration (principally to the U.S.A. and Latin America, and later Australia). The presence of immigrants in Italy's cities is a relatively new phenomenon and many Italians are still coming to terms with it.

REGIONS AND CITIES

Region	Capital
Valle d'Aosta	Aosta
Piemonte (Piedmont)	Torino (Turin)
Lombardia (Lombardy)	Milano (Milan)
Trentino-Alto Adige	Trento
Veneto	Venezia (Venice)
Friuli-Venezia Giulia	Trieste
Liguria	Genova (Genoa)
Emilia-Romagna	Bologna
Toscana (Tuscany)	Firenze (Florence)
Umbria	Perugia
Marche	Ancona
Lazio	Roma (Rome)
Abruzzi	L'Aquila
Molise	Campobasso
Campania	Napoli (Naples)
Puglia	Bari
Basilicata	Potenza
Calabria	Catanzaro
Sicilia (Sicily)	Palermo
Sardegna (Sardinia)	Cagliari

Italy contains two mini-states, the Republic of San Marino and the Vatican. San Marino covers just 24 square miles (61 sq km), and is the world's oldest (and second smallest) republic, dating from the fourth century CE. The Vatican City, a tiny enclave in the heart of Rome, is the seat of the Pope, head of the Roman Catholic Church.

The Vatican City (*Stato della Città del Vaticano*)
Measuring 109 acres (0.4 sq km), less than a third of the size of Monaco, the Vatican is a sovereign state on the west bank of the Tiber. This tiny area is what remains of the Papal States, which were created by Pope Innocent II (1198–1216) by playing off rival candidates for the title of Holy Roman Emperor. Before their conquest by the Piedmontese in the 1860s, the Papal States stretched from the Tyrrhenian Sea in the west to the Adriatic in the east, and had a population of three million souls. Today the Vatican is the world's smallest state, with an army of Swiss Guards (actually mainly Italians on temporary posting), and a population of about a thousand. Most of the workers in the Vatican City live outside and commute in every working day. As a state, it has all it needs: a post office, a railway station, a helipad, a TV and radio station broadcasting in thirty-nine languages, a bank, a hospital, refectories, drugstores, and gas stations.

The authority of the Vatican was established in 380 CE when the primacy of the Holy See—the jurisdiction of the Bishop of Rome—was officially recognized by the Western Church. As a result

Rome is the "Eternal City" to 850 million Roman Catholics worldwide. Paradoxically, in 1985 a Concordat was signed under which Catholicism ceased to be Italy's state religion.

The glories of the Vatican City are its museum, which houses the Sistine Chapel and countless works of art, and St. Peter's Basilica. This can seat a 60,000-member congregation and is 611 feet (186 meters) long, 462 feet (140 meters) wide, and 393 feet (120 meters) high. Built between 1506 and 1615, its magnificent dome and the

square Greek-cross plan were designed by Michelangelo, who worked on it "for the love of God and piety"—in other words, without pay! St. Peter's houses Michelangelo's *Pietà* (the statue of the seated Virgin holding the limp body of the dead Christ), and Bernini's bronze canopy (*baldacchino*) over the high altar.

At the head of the Vatican administration is the Pope, aided by his state secretariat under the Secretary of State. There are ten congregations, or departments, dealing with clerical matters, each headed by a cardinal. The most important is the Congregation for the Doctrine of the Faith, formerly the Inquisition. All Catholic bishops are enjoined to go to Rome at least once every five years to see the Pope "at the threshold of the apostles."

The leading sacred establishment in the Vatican is the Curia, or College of Cardinals, which comprises 120 bishops or archbishops. After the death of a Pope the electors meet in conclave and are locked into the Sistine Chapel until a new Pope is elected. After each vote, the ballots are burned and black smoke drifts up from the Sistine Chapel chimncy. When a new Pope has been elected, a chemical is added to the ballot papers to turn the smoke white, and the new Pope in his papal regalia appears to the public in the piazza. He is crowned the following day in St. Peters.

Rome
With a population of 3.8 million, Rome is Italy's capital and the seat of government. Though situated in the center of Italy, Rome is regarded as a "Southern" city in its style and general outlook.

Milan
With a population of 1.6 million and situated in the northern region of Lombardy, Milan is Italy's "New York." Sometimes described by its citizens as the real capital, Milan is the industrial center of Italy and home to two of its most famous football teams, Inter Milan and AC Milan. It is also the seat of Italy's *Borsa*, or Stock Exchange.

Naples

One of the busiest ports in Italy and the "capital" of the South, Naples has a population of just over a million. It is the jumping off point for visits to the towns of Pompeii and Herculaneum, preserved by the lava that buried them after the eruption of Mount Vesuvius in 79 CE, and for visits to the islands of Capri and Ischia.

Turin

The capital of Piedmont, Turin (pop. over 1 million) is the gateway to the Italian Alps and a major industrial center and transportation junction.

Palermo

Founded by the Phoenicians in the eighth century BC, Palermo (pop. 730,000) is the capital and chief seaport of Sicily.

Bologna

This industrial city and ancient university town (pop. 730,000) is the capital of Emilia-Romagna. It is famous for the quality of its food and is also a transportation center and agricultural market.

Genoa

Genoa (pop. 706,000), the capital of Liguria in the northwest, is Italy's largest port and a leading industrial and commercial center.

Florence

The capital of Tuscany, Florence (pop. 461,000) is famous for its architectural and artistic treasures, dating from its heyday as the leading architectural city of the Italian Renaissance under the Medici. Today it is also a fashion center and a major commercial, transportation, and industrial hub.

Venice

Capital of the Veneto region, Venice (pop. 274,580, including the mainland) is the other great Renaissance center. The old city is built on piles on islands in a saltwater lagoon, and is famous for its canals and bridges. It is both a leading cultural and architectural attraction and a major port.

A BRIEF HISTORY

Italy is renowned for its magnificent art treasures and breathtaking scenery. Two of its greatest admirers were the nineteenth-century Romantic poets Percy Bysshe Shelley and Lord Byron, both of whom lived there. Shelley, who was drowned in a storm in a small boat off the coast, near La Spezia, described Italy as "Thou paradise of exiles" (*Julian and Maddolo*, 1819), and Byron in a letter to

Annabella Milbanke on April 28, 1814, wrote "Italy is my magnet." Almost a century later, Henry James wrote to Edith Wharton, "How incomparably the old coquine of an Italy is the most beautiful country in the world—of a beauty (and an interest and complexity of beauty) so far beyond any other that none other is worth talking about."

Interestingly, Italians, from the late medieval poets Boccaccio and Dante onward, describe their country very differently. Over the centuries Italy has been depicted as a whore, a fallen woman, or even a brothel. Many of Italy's contemporary problems derive from its history as a land of separate, warring city-states, later ruled by other European powers. Italy was not unified until 1861 and in a sense still has the feeling of a "young" country, despite its antiquity.

Prehistory
In the Bronze Age, from about 2000 BCE, Italy was settled by Indo-European Italic tribes from the

Danube basin. The first indigenous sophisticated civilization was that of the Etruscans, which developed in the city-states of Tuscany. In 650 BCE Etruscan civilization expanded into central and northern Italy, setting an early example of urban living. The Etruscans controlled the seas on either side of the peninsula, and for a while provided the ruling dynasties in neighboring Latium, the lowlands in the central part of Italy's western coast. Etruscan ambitions were eventually checked by the Greeks at Cumae near Naples in 524 BCE, and the Etruscan navy was defeated by the Greeks in a sea battle off Cumae in 474 BCE.

At about this time, Greek colonies in Southern Italy were introducing the olive, the vine, and the written alphabet. Greek civilization would, of course, have a major influence on the future Roman Empire.

The Rise of Rome

During the fourth and third centuries BCE Rome, the leading city-state of Latium, rose to prominence and united the Italian peninsula under its rule. Legend has it that Rome was founded by Romulus and Remus, twin sons of the god Mars and the King of Alba Longa's daughter. Left to die near the River Tiber, the abandoned babes were suckled by a she-wolf until

they were discovered by a shepherd, who brought them up. Eventually Romulus founded Rome in 753 BCE on the Palatine Hill above the banks of the Tiber where the wolf had rescued them. He was to become the first in a line of seven kings.

Following the expulsion of its last Etruscan king, Rome became a republic in 510 BCE. Its political dominance was underpinned by its remarkably stable constitutional development, and eventually all of Italy gained full Roman citizenship. The defeat of foreign enemies and rivals led first to the establishment of protectorates and then the outright annexation of territories beyond Italy.

The Roman Empire

The Republic's victorious march across the known world continued despite political upheavals and civil war, culminating in the murder of Julius Caesar in 44 BCE and the establishment of the Roman Empire under Augustus and his

successors. Thereafter Rome flourished. Augustus famously "found Rome in brick and left it in marble." The city was burned down in 64 CE during the reign of the Emperor Nero, who, to deflect the blame, initiated a period of persecutions of Christians. It is around this time that

Saints Peter and Paul were executed. Peter was crucified upside down, whereas Paul—a Roman citizen by birth—was beheaded.

The Roman Empire lasted until the fifth century CE, and at its peak extended from Britain in the west to Mesopotamia and the Caspian Sea in the east. The Mediterranean effectively became an inland lake—*mare nostrum,* "our sea." The civilization of ancient Rome and Italy took root and had a profound influence on the development of the whole of Western Europe through the Middle Ages, the Renaissance, and beyond—in art and architecture, literature, law, and engineering, and through the international use of its language, Latin, by scholars and at the great courts of Europe.

The Fall of the Empire and the Rise of the Church

In 330 CE Constantine, the first Christian emperor, moved his capital to Byzantium (renamed Constantinople—modern-day Istanbul), and Rome declined in importance. In 395 the Empire was divided into eastern and western parts, each ruled by its own emperor. There was continuous pressure along the borders as barbarian tribes probed the overstretched imperial defenses. In 410 Rome was sacked by Visigoths from Thrace, led by Alaric. Further incursions into Italy were made by the Huns under Attila in 452, and the Vandals who sacked Rome in 455. In 476 the last western Emperor, Romulus Augustus, was deposed, and in 568 Italy was invaded by the Lombards, who occupied Lombardy and central Italy.

With the collapse of the Roman Empire in the west, the Church in Rome became the sole heir and transmitter of imperial culture and legitimacy, and the power of the papacy grew. Pope Gregory I (590–604) built four of the city's basilicas and also sent missionaries to convert pagans to Christianity (including St. Augustine to Britain). On Christmas Day 800, at a ceremony in Rome, Pope Leo III (795–816) crowned the champion of Christendom, the Frankish king Charlemagne, Emperor of the Romans, and Italy was briefly united with Germany in a new Christian Roman Empire. From then until 1250, relations between the papacy and the Holy Roman Empire, at first friendly but later hostile, were the main issue in Italian history.

The City-States

In the twelfth and thirteenth centuries Western Christendom's spiritual and temporal powers, the papacy and the Holy Roman Empire, competed for supremacy. During this struggle the Italian cities seized the opportunity to become self-governing republics. Supported by the papacy, the Northern cities formed the Lombard League to resist the Emperors' claims of sovereignty. Papal power and influence reached their peak under Pope Innocent III (1198–1216).

Italy became a jigsaw of kingdoms, duchies, and city-states running from the Alps to Sicily. Centuries of war and trade barriers fanned animosity between neighboring Italians and reinforced local loyalties. With the exception of the territory of Rome, ruled by the Pope, most of these states succumbed to foreign rule. Each preserved its own distinct government and customs and vernacular. Italian history was marked less by political achievements than by achievements in the human sphere. The great cities and medieval centers of learning were founded in this period—the University of Bologna, founded in the twelfth century, is Europe's oldest.

The Italian Renaissance

The fourteenth century saw the beginnings of the Italian Renaissance, the great cultural explosion that found sublime expression in learning and the arts. In the move from a religious to a more secular worldview, Humanism—the "new learning" of the

age—rediscovered the civilization of classical antiquity; it explored the physical universe and placed the individual at its center. Boccaccio and Petrarch wrote major works in Italian rather than Latin. In painting and sculpture, the quest for knowledge led to greater naturalism and interest in anatomy and perspective, recorded in the treatises of the artist-philosopher Leon Battista Alberti.

During this period the arts were sponsored by Italy's wealthy ruling families such as the Medici in Florence, the Sforzas in Milan, and the Borgias in Rome. This was the age of the "universal man"—polymaths and artistic geniuses such as Leonardo da Vinci, whose studies included painting, architecture, science, and engineering, and Michelangelo, who was not only a sculptor and painter, but also an architect and a poet. Other great artists were Raphael and Titian. Architects such as Brunelleschi and Bramante studied the buildings of ancient Rome to achieve balance, clarity, and proportion in their works. Andrea Palladio adapted the principles of classical architecture to the requirements of the age, creating the Palladian style.

Andreas Vesalius, who made dissection of the human body an essential part of medical studies, taught anatomy at Italian universities. The composer Giovanni Palestrina was the master of Renaissance counterpoint, at a time when Italy was the source culture of European music. Galileo Galilei produced seminal work in physics and astronomy before being arrested by the Inquisition in 1616 and obliged to recant his advocacy of the Copernican view of the solar system in 1633.

The invention of printing and the geographical voyages of discovery gave further impetus to the Renaissance spirit of inquiry and scepticism. In its bid to halt the spread of Protestantism and heterodoxy, however, the Counter-Reformation almost extinguished intellectual freedom in sixteenth-century Italy.

Foreign Invasions
In the fifteenth century most of Italy was ruled by five rival states—the city-republics of Milan, Florence, and Venice in the north; the Papal Sates in the center; and the southern Kingdom of the Two Sicilies (Sicily and Naples having been united in 1442). Their wars and rivalries laid them open to invasions from France and Spain. In 1494 Charles VIII of France invaded Italy to claim the Neapolitan crown. He was forced to withdraw by

a coalition of Milan, Venice, Spain, and the Holy Roman Empire.

In the sixteenth and seventeenth centuries Italy became an arena for the dynastic struggles of the ruling families of France, Austria, and Spain. After the defeat of France by Spain at Pavia, the Pope hastily put together an alliance against the Spaniards. The Habsburg Emperor Charles V defeated him and in 1527 his German mercenaries sacked Rome and stabled their horses in the Vatican. For some modern historians this act symbolizes the end of the Renaissance in Italy.

Spain was the new world power in the sixteenth century, and the Spanish Habsburgs dominated Italy. Charles V, who was both King of Spain and Archduke of Austria, ruled Naples and Sicily. In the seventeenth century Italy was effectively part of the Spanish Empire, and went into economic and cultural decline. After the Treaty of Utrecht in 1713, Austria replaced Spain as the dominant power, though the Kingdom of Naples came under Spanish Bourbon rule in 1735, leaving a profound influence on the culture of the South.

French Rule

The old order was swept aside by the French revolutionary wars. In the years 1796–1814 Napoleon Bonaparte conquered Italy, setting up satellite states and introducing the principles of the

French Revolution. At first he divided Italy into a number of puppet republics. Later, after his rise to absolute power in France, he gave the former Kingdom of the Two Sicilies to his brother Joseph, who became King of Naples. (This later passed to his brother-in-law Joachim Murat.) The Northern territories of Milan and Lombardy were incorporated into a new Kingdom of Italy, with Napoleon as King and his stepson Eugène Beauharnais ruling as Viceroy.

Italians under direct French rule were subject to the jurisdiction of the Code Napoleon, and became accustomed to a modern, centralized state and an individualistic society. In the Kingdom of Naples feudal privileges were abolished, and ideas of democracy and social equality were implanted. So although the period of French rule in Italy was short-lived, its legacy was a taste for political liberty and social equality, and a new-found sense of national patriotism.

In creating the Kingdom of Italy, Napoleon brought together for the first time most of the independent city-states in the northern and central parts of the peninsula, and stimulated the desire for a united Italy. At the same time, in the South there arose the revolutionary secret society of the *Carbonari* ("Charcoal-burners"), which aimed to free Italy from foreign control and secure constitutional government.

The Unification of Italy

After Napoleon's fall in 1815, the victorious Allies sought to restore the balance of power in Europe. Italy was again divided between Austria (Lombardy-Venetia), the Pope, the kingdoms of Sardinia and Naples, and four smaller duchies. However, the genie was out of the bottle. Nationalist and democratic ideals remained alive and found expression in the movement for Italian unity and independence called the *Risorgimento* ("Resurrection"). In 1831 the utopian radical Giuseppe Mazzini founded a movement called "Young Italy," which campaigned widely for a unified republic. His most celebrated disciple was the flamboyant Giuseppe Garibaldi, who had started his long revolutionary career in South America. The chief architect of the *Risorgimento*, however, was Count Camillo Cavour, the liberal Prime Minister of the Kingdom of Sardinia.

The repressive regimes imposed on Italy inspired revolts in Naples and Piedmont in 1820–21, in the Papal States, Parma, and Modena in 1831, and throughout the peninsula in 1848–49. These were suppressed everywhere except in the constitutional monarchy of Sardinia, which became the champion of Italian nationalism. Cavour's patient and skillful diplomacy won over British and French support for the struggle against absolutism. With the help of Napoleon III, Victor Emmanuel II of Sardinia expelled the Austrians from Lombardy in 1859. The following year, Garibaldi and his army of 1,000 volunteers (known as "*I Mille,*" the Thousand in Italian, or the Red Shirts) landed in Sicily. Welcomed as liberators by the people, they swept aside the despotic Bourbon dynasty and made their way north up the peninsula.

Victor Emmanuel then entered the Papal States and the two victorious armies met at Naples, where Garibaldi handed over the command of his troops to his monarch. On March 17, 1861, Victor Emmanuel was proclaimed King of Italy at Turin. Venice and part of Venetia were secured by another war with Austria in 1866, and in 1870 Italian forces occupied Rome, in defiance of the Pope, thus completing the unification of Italy. The spiritual autonomy of the Pope was recognized by the Law of Guarantees, which also gave him the status of a reigning monarch over a certain number of buildings in Rome. The Vatican became a self-governing state within Italy.

With the passing of the heroes of the *Risorgimento,* the national government in Rome became associated with corruption and inefficiency. A sense that Italy's unity had been made possible largely by its enemy's enemies (France and Prussia) and real economic hardship led to demoralization and serious unrest. There were bread riots in Milan in 1898, followed by crackdowns on socialist movements. Against this backdrop, in 1900 King Umberto I was assassinated by an anarchist.

Italy now entered the arena of European power politics and started to entertain colonial ambitions. Thwarted by France in Tunis, Italy joined Germany and Austria in the Triple Alliance in 1882 and occupied Eritrea, making it a colony in 1889. An attempt to seize Abyssinia (Ethiopia) was decisively defeated at Adowa in 1896. However, war with Turkey in 1911–12 brought Libya and the Dodecanese islands in the Aegean, and dreams of the rebirth of a glorious overseas Roman Empire. On the outbreak of the First World War, Italy denounced the Triple Alliance and remained neutral, but in 1915 entered on the side of the Allies. The treaties of 1919, however, awarded Italy far less than it demanded—Trieste, the Trentino, and South Tyrol, but, importantly, very little in the colonial sphere. This humiliation would rankle for years to come.

The postwar period in Italy saw intense political and social unrest, which the universally despised governments were too weak to subdue. Patriotic disappointment with the outcome of the war was swelled by the existence of large numbers of ex-servicemen. In 1919 the nationalist poet and aviator Gabriele D'Annunzio led an unofficial army to seize the Croatian port of Fiume, awarded to Yugoslavia under the Treaty of Versailles. Although the coup collapsed after three months, it proved to be a dress rehearsal for the Fascist takeover four years later.

The March on Rome

In the following years inflation, unemployment, riots, and crime were rife. Workers' soviets were set up in factories. Socialists and Communists marched through the streets. Against this background, the "clean sweep" offered by Benito Mussolini's right-wing populist Fascist movement appealed widely to the threatened middle classes, industrialists, and landowners, and to patriots of all classes. Its insignia was the ancient Roman symbol of authority, the *fasces*—an ax surrounded by rods tightly bound together for strength and security. Electoral gains in 1921 led to growing arrogance and violence, and squads of armed Fascists attacked and terrorized their enemies in the big towns.

In October 1922 the fiery young Mussolini addressed thousands of black-shirted followers at a rally in Naples demanding the handover of government; the crowd responded with chants of

"*Roma, Roma, Roma.*" The Fascist militias mobilized. Luigi Facta, the last constitutional Prime Minister, resigned, and thousands of Blackshirts, or "*Camicie Nere,*" marched on Rome unopposed. King Victor Emmanuel III appointed Mussolini Prime Minister, and Italy entered a dangerous new era.

The Fascist Years

Mussolini moved quickly to secure the loyalty of the army. Critically, he reconciled the Italian state with the estranged Vatican, signing a solemn Concordat with the Pope in 1929 that conferred authority on his government. Although technically still a constitutional monarchy, Italy was now a dictatorship. The Fascist regime brutally destroyed all opposition, and exerted almost complete control over every facet of Italian life. In the early years, despite the suppression of individual liberties, it won wide acceptance by improving the administration, stabilizing the economy, improving workers' conditions, and inaugurating a program of public

works. Italy's man of destiny, *il Duce* ("the Leader"), was idolized and came to embody the corporate state. There are obvious parallels with Adolf Hitler's regime in Germany. Unlike the Nazis, however, Fascist doctrine did not include a theory of racial purity. Anti-Semitic measures were introduced only in 1938, probably under German pressure, and were never followed through in anything like the German manner.

Mussolini saw himself as heir to the Roman emperors, and aggressively set about building an empire. The well-equipped Italian army sent to conquer Ethiopia in 1935–36 used poison gas and bombed Red Cross hospitals. When threatened with sanctions, Italy joined Nazi Germany in the Axis alliance of 1936. In April 1939 Italy invaded Albania, whose king fled, after which Victor Emmanuel was proclaimed King of Italy and Albania, and Emperor of Ethiopia. Naturally supportive of fellow dictators, Mussolini intervened on the side of General Franco's nationalist forces in the Spanish Civil War (1936–39), and entered the Second World War as an ally of Germany.

The war did not go well for Italy. Defeats in North Africa and Greece, the Allied invasion of Sicily, and discontent at home destroyed Mussolini's prestige. He was forced to resign by his own Fascist Council in 1943. The new Italian government under Marshal Badoglio surrendered to the Allies and declared war on Germany. Rescued by German parachutists, Mussolini established a breakaway government in northern

Italy. The Germans occupied northern and central Italy, and until its final liberation in 1945 the country was a battlefield. Mussolini and his mistress, Clara Petacci, were captured by Italian partisans at Lake Como while trying to flee the country, and shot. Their bodies were hung upside down in a public square in Milan.

POSTWAR ITALY

In 1946 Victor Emmanuel abdicated in favor of his son, Umberto II, who reigned for thirty-four days. In a referendum in June, Italians voted (by 12 million to 10 million) to abolish the monarchy, and Italy became a republic. It was stripped of its colonies in 1947. A new constitution came into force the following year, and the Christian Democrats emerged as the party of government.

The new monarch abdicated and, with all members of the house of Savoy, was forbidden to reenter the country. (In May 2003 the Senate voted by 235 to 19 to allow the royal family, the Savoia, to return to Italy.)

In attempting to weld the peninsula's separate entities into a single unified kingdom, Italy's early leaders had created a highly bureaucratic state that was tailor-made for Mussolini to manipulate fifty years later. This overcentralized system run from Rome survived the downfall of Fascism and the end of the discredited monarchy, but it landed the fledgling republic with a huge and costly bureaucracy and antiquated mechanisms for decision-making.

For most of the second half of the twentieth century, Italy was governed by an increasingly corrupt Christian Democrat–Liberal–Socialist coalition. Endless power struggles within the coalition caused governments to collapse and reconstitute themselves with notorious regularity, but the regime was assumed to be a fixture. Since it was a powerful source of patronage, its excesses remained unchecked until the early 1990s, when scandalous revelations of graft at all levels of politics and big business caused the Christian Democrat majority to wither away overnight. For the Italians, this was almost as momentous an event as the end of the Soviet Empire.

The darkest period in Italy's postwar history, echoes of which can be heard even today, were the *anni di piombo*, or "Years of Lead." During what 'Co – 80a one Italian journalist described as a low-intensity civil war in the 1960s, there were 15,000 terrorist attacks in which 491 Italians were killed, including leading politicians such as the Christian Democrat leader Aldo Moro. The *anni di piombo* lasted right up to the early 1980s and spawned a number of notorious groups such as the Red Brigades (*Brigate Rosse*), and atrocities by left-wing activists such as the explosion in Piazza Fontana in Milan in 1969. In this period Italy was plagued by crime from both left and right.

The Mafia, the traditional source of organized crime in Italy, originating in Sicily, controlled local politicians and businesses, often with considerable internal violence, and assassinated judges and politicians who resisted them. (In Sicily the Mafia is known as the Cosa Nostra; its Neapolitan counterpart is the Camorra.)

The *Mani Pulite* Campaign

The 1990s saw the *Mani Pulite*, or "Clean Hands," anticorruption campaign to clean up public life. Although there is a degree of cynicism about the results, the campaign marked a break with the violent extremist politics of the '60s and '70s and the emergence of a more mainstream government. After major electoral reforms, the 1996 elections were a fight between the old-established opposition parties and a cluster of newcomers, the ex-Communists and their allies versus a hastily assembled right-wing coalition consisting of the reformed neo-Fascists, a rapidly growing Northern separatist party (the Lega Nord, also known just as the Lega), and Forza Italia, led by the media tycoon (and one of the world's richest men) Silvio Berlusconi. For fifty years after the Second World War, Italy had succeeded in keeping its two extremes, Fascism and Communism, out of national government. The Communists were the second-largest and best-organized party in Italy but were excluded due to the Cold War fear of Marxism. The neo-Fascists were still seen as too closely associated with memories of the rule of Mussolini.

Now the old antagonists have changed their images and today both right and left are trying to present themselves as "mainstream." The ex-Communists (rebaptized Partito Democratico della Sinistra, or PDS) were the leading players in the center-left coalition that led the country after 1996 and presided over the stringent fiscal reforms that enabled Italy to join the European Monetary Union in January 1999.

The Age of Berlusconi

In the 2001 elections, Silvio Berlusconi, head of Mediaset and a range of other international and national business interests, and leader of the Forza Italia coalition in the Italian Parliament, became Prime Minister. The following year, Italy held the presidency of the European Union.

GOVERNMENT

Under its constitution, Italy is a multiparty republic with an elected president as Head of

State and a prime minister as Head of Government. There are two legislative bodies, a 325-seat Senate and a 633-seat Chamber of Deputies. Elections are held every five years. The prime minister is the leader of the party or coalition that wins the election. The country is divided administratively into twenty regions that reflect to a considerable degree its traditional regional customs and character.

POLITICS

Politics in Italy is confrontational, and at street level has sometimes been murderous, but in the end it is always about the art of accommodation.

Some Italian cities such as Bologna are famous for their left-wing politics, and the large and prosperous center-north "red" regions of Tuscany, Emilia-Romagna, and Marche have a long Communist tradition. Over the years, however, Italian politics has become more centrist, and the country is settling into an alternation of center-left and center-right coalitions.

Apart from competing ideologies, when two strong personalities within a political party clash, the loser often starts another party, which then becomes part of one of the major coalitions.

Today in Italian politics, television is king and the center-right bloc is dominated by Silvio

Berlusconi, whose Mediaset conglomerate owns half of Italy's TV and publishing industry and a top football team, AC Milan. Despite (or perhaps because of) extensive charges of corruption and tax scams, this self-made billionaire, calling for tax cuts and deregulation, is the hero of many of Italy's small businessmen and entrepreneurs, not to mention soccer fans and TV addicts.

ECONOMIC LIFE

Fifty years ago, Italy was a largely agrarian society. It is now the fifth- or sixth-biggest manufacturing economy in the world. Even today, however, it is characterized by great disparities of income. Pockets of great wealth and industry, such as Milan, are in marked contrast to areas with a far lower standard of living, particularly in the South (known as the *Mezzogiorno*), where patron/client relationships are still common. Lombardy alone accounts for 20 percent of Italy's GDP.

Although visited for its historic art treasures, Italy strikes the visitor as a modern nation in a continuing state of evolution. It is a relatively young nation, too. This is often reflected in a "get rich quick" mentality of unrestrained commercialism. Many areas of natural beauty have been ruined by indiscriminate property development, particularly along the coasts.

chapter two

VALUES & ATTITUDES

Italy's geographical structure and historical divisions have produced a country of distinct regions, each with its own dialect, politics, and culture. For this reason one feature dominates Italian life—the family.

FAMILY FIRST

The importance of family in Italian life cannot be overestimated. Your family are the people you can trust, the people you work for, the people you do favors for or who do favors for you. The most extreme example of "family first" is probably the Sicilian Mafia, whose code of honor permits vendettas or revenge killings between families lasting generations and whose loyalty is based entirely on the family.

At an everyday level, the Italians love talking about families and regard the family as giving you roots and a stake in society. It is always useful to carry photos of your family with you (if you don't have one, invent one!) to show around and discuss. It is one of the best ways of creating links with Italians.

Business in Italy is still dominated by family firms, with the sons or daughters of the founder frequently taking over and running the business. The Italians take family seriously and if they have known you since they were young, then you too are part of their family. When one foreign company ended its agency contract with its Italian distributor after years of unsuccessful performance, the distraught head of the Italian firm protested, "But I've known you since I was four! I sat on my father's knee while he negotiated with you." The implication was, "How could you do this to a member of your family?"

FEELINGS AND EMOTIONS

Italians are "feeling" people. They readily accept and exchange information, but ultimately decisions are made on gut feeling, with family and regional considerations also playing an important role. This means that the way they look at things tends to be particular and subjective. Rather than apply universal rules, an Italian will look at the details of each situation and decide each one on its (or your) merits. That is why, whatever the rule, there is always an exception if you can make a case for it.

This is not to say that facts have no place in Italian life, but they will always be considered in relation to the people concerned. This attitude may even bind people together who are poles apart politically. It is perfectly possible to have extreme left-wing and extreme right-wing views within the same family but this does not prevent communication. What characterizes Italian society, as American author Terri Morrison points out in *Kiss, Bow or Shake Hands*, is a strong capacity for social and cultural resilience and continuity.

THE CHURCH

Although Italy is not officially a Catholic country, the Catholic Church still has an important role in providing a structure to Italian life. Whether in opposition to it or in sympathy with it, the Church provides a focus for values and attitudes, and has shaped Italian culture. Religion is still a part of everyday life for large numbers of Italians.

The authority of the Catholic Church rests upon the apostolic succession—the belief that Christ ordained St. Peter, his successor on earth, who became the first Bishop of Rome. The Pope's word, when spoken *ex cathedra* (from his throne), is considered to be God's law.

It is impossible to overestimate the

importance of the Catholic tradition in people's daily lives, whether or not they profess to being believers or are practicing Christians. Life in Italy is to a degree influenced by your belief in or opposition to the Catholic hierarchy. Catholicism is an autocratic, top-down religion, with a hierarchy of authority extending from the Pope, down through the cardinals, archbishops, and bishops to the local parish priest. This hierarchical approach is reflected in society in the authority of the father, the structure of Italian business, the artistic culture of the people, and the church bells summoning the faithful to mass.

TOLERANCE

On the other hand, the Italians are remarkably tolerant of moral lapses that the Catholic Church finds unacceptable. So petty crime, fraud, and sexual infidelity are, if not accepted, recognized as examples of human frailty and overlooked. After all, who has not sinned at some time? The important thing is to keep up appearances at all times and at all costs. This means that Italians can be astonishingly flexible and understanding in difficult situations. A foreign middleman once drew up a contract incorrectly. Afraid of being sued by both sides, he asked his Italian counterpart if it would be possible to draw up a new one. "No problem," said the Italian. "Just give me the new contract, I'll sign it and tear up the old one. After all, we all make mistakes."

BELLA FIGURA

In Britain it's humor, in France it's ideas, in Germany it's respectability, and in Italy it's appearances that make the world go round. It's true that in Italy how you dress and act speaks volumes about you and it's important to dress and act correctly. "When in Rome, do as the Romans do," goes the popular saying, and the Romans, like all Italians, set great store by making a *bella figura*.

In a country with so many fine fashion houses, and where individuals can seem very assertive, looking good and making the right impression is paramount. The Italians, especially women, spend a small fortune on clothes and place importance on the right designer labels. So a cyclist dresses like a champion and dress rivalry starts in nursery school. Italians claim they can spot foreigners from a mile off not only by what they wear but by how they wear it—if you protest that this is a victory of style over substance, Italians will retort that their style is part of the substance. So cutting a *bella figura* is important for visitor and businessperson alike.

This means that many problems in Italy are

seen as less a matter of corruption or poor management than as poor presentation. *Fare una brutta figura* is to make a bad impression. To make a *good* impression, it is important to show off. People admire *ricchezza* (wealth) and *bellezza* (beauty). Putting on a good face to disguise a bad performance is admired. So much of Italy is a beautiful presentation, rather like a swan gliding across the surface of the water while its legs paddle furiously beneath.

LOUDNESS

Italy is traditionally noisy. Life is lived much more in public than in Britain or the U.S.A., and private conversations can be easily overheard in the piazzas and streets. Added to this is the incessant roar of the cars and the hooting of the mopeds (*motorini*). The noise of conversation or shouted commands mingling with the sound of traffic takes some getting used to, but as at least one observer—the English author Tobias Jones in *The Dark Heart of Italy*—notes, "After a while, other countries begin to seem eerily quiet, even dull."

A characteristic of Italy is the verbal jousting as people exchange lively opinions and even criticisms in earthy, uninhibited language. It feels as if reserve and reticence have fallen away and been replaced by vivacity and sensuousness, a quality that the English writer D. H. Lawrence termed "blood knowledge."

ORDER AND HIERARCHY

Italy's strong sense of hierarchy and formality, as Tobias Jones found, is reflected in the language. "*Ciao*," the ubiquitous way of saying "Hi" and "Good-bye," is derived from *schiavo*, meaning "slave." If you go into a shop in Venice, the shopkeeper will say, "*Comandi*," or "Command me." To do all kinds of things in Italy you need to obtain permission, "*chiedere il permesso*," either informally or by the grant of a *permesso* (permit), and a situation often needs to be *sistemato* (systematized, or sorted out). *Tutto a posto*, "everything in its place," is not perhaps what you naturally expect to be an Italian ideal.

One aspect of hierarchy is the deference paid to Italy's first families, *il salotto buono*, who run the country's key industries and who have a huge influence on politics as well as business. Following the Italian penchant for nicknames, all have their pet public titles: Gianni Agnelli, the owner of Fiat, was known as *l'Avvocato* (the Lawyer), Carlo de Benedetti, media mogul and owner of *Repubblica*, is known as *l'Ingegnere* (the Engineer), and Silvio

Berlusconi, Prime Minister and owner of Mediaset, is known variously as *il Cavaliere* (the Cavalier) and *Sua Emittenza* (His Emittance, in an ironic combination of a Cardinal's title, His Eminence, with the idea of a mass-media tycoon whose stations emit broadcasts).

The Italian way is top-down, authoritarian. As an Italian associate of an international legal firm explained, "The senior partner is God. He takes all the decisions. I am there to obey." This sense of hierarchy emanates from Church and state and bureaucracy and influences both family and social life. It is made acceptable by *garbo*, and by a sense of responsibility for personal lives, and also by a tolerance of human foibles and mistakes.

GARBO

This search for order is systematized in *garbo*, which can be translated as graciousness, courtesy, politeness, good manners. It describes the ability to calm or smooth over difficult situations, usually by the use of elaborate language.

Derived from the Arabic greeting, "*Salaam Aleikum*," the *salamelecco* is the ability to use obsequious, even groveling language to obtain something from officials. To the Americans and the British, who are used to being more concise, this can be a challenge. By comparison, the

Italians tend to see the British and the Americans as rather brutal and to-the-point. The expressive, courteous way of communicating in Italian means it can be very difficult to get to the point of a conversation; and it may also mean that the real issues are hidden or confused.

RELATIONSHIPS

In Italian business and social life everything depends on relationships and who you know. (More on this in Chapter 8, Business Briefing.) At any level, the way to get things done is to be introduced by a common friend, associate, or acquaintance. This *raccomandazione*, or recommendation, is vital to both business and social life. It will not necessarily ensure acceptance—that will depend on your own personal qualities—but a *raccomandazione* will ensure that you make the initial contact and are treated with consideration.

The other side of the coin is that your Italian colleagues will expect regular contact, consideration, and participation from you. Friendship needs to be worked at—contacting someone only when you need support or have something to offer is simply not enough. Once you have an Italian friend or associate it is a lifelong family relationship, not just an arm's-length cordial agreement. To be a friend of an Italian means being welcomed not just into their family but also into their community.

CAMPANILISMO AND THE PIAZZA

The Italians are local people and devoted to their community. The piazza is the symbolic center of a town and the seat of civic pride. It is close to a similar concept, *campanilismo* (literally, affection for one's own bell tower), or local patriotism. The Italians identify much more readily with their local area than with the rather amorphous state, which is often seen as an outside exploiter largely run by Southerners. Most Italians would like to live and work near where they were born.

However, millions of Italians from Sicily and the South have emigrated to the northern part of the country, and overseas to Australia and the United States. But people don't forget their local roots, their local cuisine, their local history, and dialect.

The writer Carlo Levi described Italy as thousands of countries, and many Italians live and work close to where they were born. Italian children live at home longer than in many other countries, and more relatives live in the same town or even under the same roof. The combination of provincialism and cosmopolitanism is one of the most attractive features of Italian life.

In conversation, therefore, it is important to value your associate's or friend's local community, food, wine and traditions. If you are presented with some local wine or *grappa* (brandy), you should express your appreciation; a visit to a favorite beauty spot or historic center is an honor, and to be given a book or souvenir of the local community is a gift to be treasured.

Though the Italians are not noticeably patriotic at the national level, they identify passionately with their local culture, region, town or city, and history. They will describe themselves as Venetians, Florentines, or Sicilians first, and as Italians afterward. One modern institution that embodies local pride is the football team.

BUREAUCRACY—THE FOURTH ESTATE

The frustrations of the Italian bureaucratic system are another reason for the average Italian's distrust of the state. According to Tobias Jones, Italy isn't so much a religious country as a clerical one. The bureaucracy has enormous importance. He cites a recent study, which suggests that the average Italian spends two working weeks of every year in lines and form-filling. Bureaucracy in Italy is time-consuming, expensive, document-heavy, and slow. It has been nicknamed the *lentocrazia*, the "slowocracy." This is partly due to Italy's long legal history. Another reason is the politicization of the Italian civil service and the fact that jobs here can be rewards for political services. A civil-service post is often called a *poltrona* (literally, armchair), "a cushy number" that means a job for life. Although civil-service jobs are now awarded on merit rather than on contacts, getting as far as the selection board may require the help of a *raccomandazione* from an important family.

Bureaucracy looms so large in the lives of Italians that an entire profession is devoted to smoothing one's way through the red tape. A *faccendiere*, or "fixer," will get you the forms, show you how to fill them in, and stand in line on your behalf. Any Italian will tell you that although most problems can be managed, a little cunning goes a long way. It pays to be *furbo*.

BEING *FURBO*

A perennial Italian preoccupation is how to beat the system: that can only be done by noncompliance until the last moment, trying to find ways of getting around laws and edicts, and generally being *furbo,* or cunning. This is the exact opposite of people who stick by the rules or play it by the book, and can cause frustration and even anger in foreigners. For an Italian, *ingenuità* doesn't mean being ingenuous but being gullible. Personal wrongdoing may be excused by comparison with the corruption that is evident at all levels of government, in the legal system, and even in the Church itself. This blatant disregard for legal constraints means the only thing you can rely on is the network of personal loyalty, which alone is the foundation of absolute trust.

Being *furbo* means looking out for yourself and your family and friends, which helps to explain the Italians' cavalier attitude to traffic lights, jaywalking, pedestrian crossings, no smoking signs, speed limits, and even the wearing of seatbelts in cars. (When Italy first made seatbelts compulsory, Naples developed a thriving trade in T-shirts with a seatbelt printed across them!) Only the rules for dining and dress seem to be rigidly observed.

CONCLUSION

The key values that can be said to distinguish Italians are their adherence to personal loyalty and friendship over any commitment to universal, state-instituted laws and regulations, and their strong commitment to the local community over and even against the state. As we have seen, Italians may be Italians to foreigners, but to other Italians they are Florentines, Venetians, Milanese, Romans, Neapolitans, or Sicilians. By upholding local customs, institutions, and traditions, they create the astonishingly rich and varied tapestry of Italian life that allows the foreigner to enjoy the distinctiveness of Venice and Rome, and to appreciate the artistic creations of both the Florentine and the Venetian schools of the Italian Renaissance, and so much more besides. The Italians themselves value their local culture and traditions, whether it be in food, wine, art and architecture, music, or drama.

chapter three

FESTIVALS &
TRADITIONS

Italy is predominantly a Catholic nation.
Although church attendance has declined
dramatically in recent years, surveys show that 80
percent of the population believe in God, and
Famiglia Cristiana (*The Christian Family*) is still
the most widely read magazine in Italy. Catholic
attitudes, stressing the importance of the family,
still count enormously.

The power of local bishops and of the Vatican,
although not overt, is immense and even if people
adopt an anticlerical stance, they are still very
aware of the influence of "the Church" in a way
that Protestants find difficult to understand.

However, the puritanism that accompanies
belief in some other Christian countries is absent
from Italy. "We are all sinners," say the Italians, so
peccadilloes such as tax evasion (engaged in by 90
percent of the population, according to official
estimates), and the millions of illegal dwellings
built in defiance of government regulations, as
well as extramarital affairs, are all unofficially
recognized as part of Italian life.

Italy enjoys Christian as well as lay public holidays, although fewer than in many other Latin countries. With its strong local and regional traditions, it also enjoys holidays associated with local areas. Every town or village has its patron saint, and on the saint's day there may well be a celebration and a day off work. Check the mayor's office or the local tourist information bureau before visiting. When a holiday falls in the middle of the week, Italians tend to "make a bridge" (*fare un ponte*) and take the extra day or two off leading into the weekend.

MAIN ITALIAN PUBLIC HOLIDAYS

DATE	FESTIVAL
January 1	New Year's Day
January 6	Epiphany
March/April	Easter Monday
April 25	Liberation Day
May 1	Labor Day
June 2	Republic Day
August 15	*Ferragosto* (Assumption Day)
November 1	All Saints
December 8	Immaculate Conception
December 25	Christmas Day
December 26	Santo Stefano

culture smart! **italy**

THE FESTIVE YEAR

Christmas

The birth of Christ is one of the two major festivals of the Christian liturgical calendar and is celebrated at home. Pine trees are erected in the main piazzas and hung with red ribbons and other decorations, shepherds from the Abruzzi mountains play their bagpipes in the streets of Rome, and Naples' historic center swarms with people buying the traditional figurines for their Christmas cribs. It is the perfect time to visit towns that are usually clogged by tourists, such as Rome, Florence, and Venice. Although Italians tend to leave the big cities to spend Christmas with their families, the tradition of eating out continues, so you can share the atmosphere of a real family Christmas meal. One warning: book first, otherwise you won't get in.

If you are in Rome over Christmas, High Mass on Christmas Day at the Vatican is a great event. After the Pope has presided over the mass, assisted by his cardinals, he addresses the faithful in the piazza in front of St. Peter's, flanked by a phalanx of *carabinieri* and the Vatican's own Swiss Guards.

New Year's Day and Epiphany

While Christmas is spent at home with the family, New Year's Eve is the time to party with friends.

For the Italians (as for the Spanish), another important festival is Twelfth Night, or Epiphany, the day the three Wise Men, or the Three Kings, visited Christ's crib in Bethlehem.

It is a custom on New Year's Eve to get rid of unwanted objects. New Year's Day is a great time to salvage good-quality discarded possessions—you may find anything from a slightly battered leather sofa to last-season's Gucci handbag.

As well as Father Christmas (known as *Babbo Natale* in Italian), Italy has the *Befana*, a little old lady, ugly but wise, who stuffs socks with sweets as presents on Epiphany.

Easter

The second-biggest festival in the Catholic Church is Easter, which celebrates the death and resurrection of Christ. Although Christmas is more widely celebrated by the general public, from a religious point of view Easter is more important.

Although Easter Monday is the official public holiday, many Italians will also take off the whole of Holy Week, or *Settimana Santa*. All over Italy there are processions and passion plays. One of the oldest is at Chieti in Abruzzo. In Taranto in Puglia on Holy Thursday, there is a procession of the Addolorata, and on Good Friday statues displaying the Passion of Christ are carried around town. At Piana degli Albanesi, near Palermo in Sicily, Easter is celebrated according to Byzantine rites and women in fifteenth-century costumes give out Easter eggs.

On Good Friday, the *Via Crucis* ("Stations of the Cross") service is held, and all votive statues and paintings in the churches are covered in black, to mark the beginning of the feast of Easter. Many practicing Catholics will have given something up for Lent (sweets, cigarettes, eating meat on Fridays). Easter Saturday is a "normal" day—the real celebration takes place on Easter Sunday, when the statues are uncovered, the churches are filled with flowers, and the church bells ring out. Easter Day is celebrated with a huge family meal, which leaves Easter Monday as a day to recover.

Liberation Day (April 25)
This celebrates the end of the German occupation in 1945. It is marked by processions through the streets and the laying of wreaths on Italian war memorials.

Labor Day (May 1)
The international day of the worker is celebrated in some Italian towns with processions organized by trade unions and political parties.

Republic Day (June 2)

This commemorates the founding of the Republic of Italy in 1946.

All Saints (November 1)

All Saints Day venerates the love and courage of all the Christian saints and martyrs. The day after (All Souls) is traditionally the day of the dead, when people go to the cemeteries to lay wreaths on family graves.

Immaculate Conception (December 8)

The festival of the Immaculate Conception, like the Assumption, demonstrates the great reverence in which the Virgin Mary is held by the Catholic Church. The feast celebrates the purity of the Virgin, who gave birth to the Son of God through divine conception, and is marked by church services and processions.

ANNUAL VACATIONS

Italians take a month's vacation every year and this tends to be in August, when most family firms close down completely—except for those in the tourist trade, which tend to take their vacations over Christmas and the New Year, so if you are visiting major cities at that time, don't be surprised if some of your guidebook's recommendations are closed. Although August is the official vacation month, things tend to slow down in July in preparation for the holiday, and are slow in picking up again in September.

A particularly popular vacation time for the Italians is the week around August 15 (the feast of the Assumption of the Virgin Mary), known as *Ferragosto*. Many shops and restaurants close from then until early September, giving Italian cities a strangely deserted air.

LOCAL HOLIDAYS

One of the unexpected results of *campanilismo* (the strong sense of local identity) is that local saint's days often become unofficial local holidays. In Parma, for example, January 13 is the feast of St. Hilary, the town's patron saint, and no one in Parma works on that day.

In the capital, Rome, additional local holidays are: April 21 (which celebrates the founding of the city by Romulus), and June 29 (the days celebrating St. Peter and St. Paul, the city's patron saints).

Italy has far too many local festivals to mention here, but two of the best-known internationally are *Carnevale* and Siena's *Palio*.

CARNEVALE

In the ten days or so before Ash Wednesday, many towns put on carnivals as one last blow-out before Lent, the six-week period of fasting and abstinence leading to Easter. The most famous is in Venice, with its masked balls and gondola processions and invitation to general licentiousness. Many celebrations in Italy hark back to the Middle Ages and are commemorated with revivals of medieval fairs, horseback sports, and costumes.

The day before Ash Wednesday is known as *Martedì Grasso* (Mardi Gras), when Venetians and visitors alike don the *bautta* (a hood and cape) and the *tabarro* (a cloak), with a tricorn hat and a white decorated mask. This allows people to go around incognito. Not everyone dresses up, but Venice is full of boutiques ready and able to sell you the gear, and you'll have a lot more fun if you join in.

THE *PALIO*

One of the most famous of the medieval throwbacks is Siena's *Palio* (literally, banner), in which members of the different quarters of the town ride bareback in a horse race around the central piazza. The event includes a parade in which their supporters in medieval costume go before them. The *Palio* takes place twice a year, on

July 2 and August 16, and is the climax of five days of rehearsals and months of preparation.

In the Middle Ages, each of Siena's seventeen *contrade*, or districts, provided a local militia to defend the city against Florence. Over the years their administrative role waned but their social influence grew. The *contrada* registers baptisms, marriages, and deaths; and many Sienese men and women are reluctant to marry outside it. The original purpose of the *Palio* was to give thanks to the Madonna, but it is really a competition

between the *contrade*, each team with its own colors and flag. The race itself lasts barely ninety seconds, but is preceded by some three hours of pageantry and parades. The winning *contrada* is presented with the banner (the *palio*), which is the prize, and each team then retires to its own neighborhood for a celebratory meal, with long tables laid out in the back streets and alleys.

NAME-DAYS

Italians often celebrate their name-days. A name-day (*onomastico*) is the feast day of the particular saint after whom someone is named. So Antonio will celebrate the day dedicated to St. Anthony of Padua, and Francesca will celebrate the day dedicated to St. Francis of Assisi, perhaps even taking the day off work and enjoying a celebratory meal with friends and family.

This is not to say that Italians don't work hard or appreciate hard work in others. But it is hard work for a specific purpose, or to get a specific job done on time to the required standard. Workaholics are not appreciated!

SAINTS

A person who is recognized as having lived a holy life, or who is notable for the manner of their death (martyrdom in defense of the Faith, for example), may become a saint in the Catholic Church. The candidate's life and background are subjected to exhaustive examination—reported miracles must be scientifically authenticated— and, if accepted, this leads, first, to beatification and then to canonization by the Pope.

Padre Pio

One of the most important candidates for sainthood in Italy in recent times was Padre Pio (1887–1968), a parish priest in San Giovanni Rotondo in the Gargano mountains of the southern region of Puglia. This is now Italy's most visited tourist spot, with 6 million visitors a year (even more popular than Lourdes in

France). His fame derives from the fact that in 1918 he became the only Catholic priest to receive the stigmata, the appearance of the bleeding wounds of Christ's crucifixion in his hands and feet. During his life and after his death, numerous unexplained events are alleged to have occurred. Padre Pio was beatified in 1999 and now awaits canonization.

BEHAVIOR IN CHURCH

Because many festivals are celebrated in church, which is also where the most magnificent art, architecture, and sculpture are to be found, it is important to be aware of the correct way to behave in a Catholic church. Clothing, first: in many churches, it is seen as disrespectful for a woman to enter wearing shorts and a low-cut top, although it is no longer necessary to cover one's head (and men should not wear a hat). So do not wander in and out of churches in shorts, sun tops, and baseball caps. You will see older women with shawls over their heads as a mark of respect.

In a Catholic church, God is always present in the host, kept in the tabernacle on the high altar or in one of the side chapels. It is denoted by a small red oil lamp left burning. You will find that many worshipers genuflect at the entrance to the nave that leads up to the altar, or when crossing in front of the altar. As you enter the church, there is always a bowl set into the wall by the door, containing holy water. Practicing Catholics will dip their fingers into it on entering and leaving the church, and make the sign of the cross.

It is important to remember that a church is a place of worship (in popular tourist sites, one area may be roped off for prayer), so a quiet, low-voiced, and respectful demeanor is appropriate.

SUPERSTITION

Where there is devotion, there is also superstition. "Italy is a land full of ancient cults, rich in natural and supernatural powers," said the Italian film director Federico Fellini, "and so everyone feels its influence. After all, whoever seeks God, finds him … wherever he wants."

Italians are addicted to superstition. Fortune-tellers are given space on national TV, and astrologers and diviners are ubiquitous. Superstitions are often specific to particular regions, arising as they do from local peasant myths and beliefs. (They are particularly strong in the South.) What they have in common is a belief in good and bad luck, and the presence of spirits.

Malocchio (pronounced "malockio;" the evil eye) is an important element in Italian superstition. Extending your little and index fingers, while

GOOD AND BAD LUCK

For a religious country like Italy, it may be surprising that it is considered unlucky to see a nun, and Italians may touch iron (their equivalent of touching wood for luck) to ward off the bad luck.

- To hear a cat sneeze is considered lucky, but to have a bird in the house is unlucky.
- Peacock feathers may be banned from the home because the big circular eye in the feather looks like "the evil eye."
- Chrysanthemums in Italy are only for graves, and they are always associated with funerals—don't take them as a present for your hostess!
- Italy's unlucky number (not strictly observed) is 17 because it is the sum of the Latin letters VIXI, which can be read as "I have lived," or "I'm now dead"! Thirteen, unlucky in most Western cultures, is considered lucky in Italy. However, 13 is still an unlucky number to have around a table, and 4 is also associated with death.
- *Gnocchi* are small round potato dumplings. Eating them on September 29 brings good luck.

keeping the others folded down, is supposed to ward off the evil spirit that someone has put on you. Some people wear a necklace or bracelet with a horn-shaped charm (*corno*) to ward off the evil eye.

Even a compliment may invoke the evil spirit. If someone praises your small son or daughter, for example, you may fear this has attracted the evil eye. Parents may make the sign of the horn over a child to protect it. One way of telling whether someone has put the evil eye on you is to pour oil into holy water—if the oil spreads, it's a good sign, but if it coagulates, you're in trouble!

A number of superstitions surround death and burial. For example, taking a coffin to the cemetery by one route and returning by another is meant to confuse the dead and avoid them returning. Putting salt under a person's head in the coffin was done for the same reason. It was common to place the deceased's favorite personal effects in the coffin and, if something was forgotten, to include it in the next burial as it could be safely assumed that both the dead would meet up in heaven.

CONCLUSION
Italy does not just have historical and religious festivals but some of Europe's most important music, drama, and film festivals as well. More about those in Chapter 6, Time Out.

chapter four

MAKING FRIENDS

The Italians are used to foreigners. Pilgrims, poets, merchants, artists, tourists, and invading armies have all made their way through the country. In the eighteenth and early nineteenth centuries no young English nobleman's education was complete without the "Grand Tour" of Europe, taking in the famous sights that tourists still flock to today. Venice, for example, has about 275,000 inhabitants, but 8 million visitors a year!

ESTEROFILIA

By and large, Italians are friendly people who are "*esterofiliac*." This describes a liking for all things foreign; it is manifested in the wide use of foreign words, particularly English words in broadcasting and sports. This is not a linguistic failure of Italian but a delight in incorporating buzzwords from other languages and Italianizing them. A football manager is "*il mister*," for example, and the terms *corner*, *dribblando* (dribbling), and *offside* are common in football commentary.

CLOSE-KNIT CIRCLES

Forming close links with Italians can be more difficult, however. The Italians are essentially local people with strong and extensive family and regional links. Their close friendships are formed when they are young and remain a tight circle all their lives. They often feel no need to reach outside it, and have difficulty understanding how anyone else doesn't have their own network.

Outside the big international cities it can be hard to break into the local community. When the English author Tim Parks and his Italian wife, Rosa, moved to a small village on the outskirts of Verona, they found it a slow and gradual process. He describes this with humor and insight in his book, *Italian Neighbours.*

Even before Tim got to know his neighbors, he paid a visit to the village *bar/pasticceria,* a habit he considers essential for anyone wishing to integrate into Italian life. Timing, he stresses, is important. Everything has its right time, and the measure of how well you've integrated is that you know when to order your *cappuccino* (before 10:30 a.m.) and your *digestivo,* or Prosecco. Pick up the local newspaper (which all bars are legally obliged to provide) to get a sense of what's going on.

Gradually, you advance and are recognized. Someone nods to you. Once they know you are a native English-speaker, you may be asked to help with a short translation. In time you will get to know your neighbors. The initial contact may be formal, but polite and kind; while Italians recognize the importance of hospitality, they prefer to retain a degree of formality at first.

Doing a service or being useful to the people in your building can help build up good relations, but remember, the Italian sense of privacy can be just as strong as that of the British. As Tim Parks observes, "If the Englishman's home is his castle, an Italian's is his bunker."

When talking to Italians, an obsession with health and doctors is a common subject. Blood pressure, visits to the doctor, and tests are all exhaustively discussed, quite often on very slight acquaintance. The superiority of all things Italian is taken as a matter of course by Italians, although they will show a polite interest in life abroad.

The initial reserve toward outsiders applies equally to Italians from "out of town." Rosa Parks' greetings of "*Buon giorno, Signore,*" or "*Buona sera, Signora,*" were met with embarrassment and silence until, eventually, nods of acknowledgment were accompanied by a return greeting.

The breakthrough, Tim found, came when his wife became pregnant. Suddenly the couple weren't fly-by-nights but people with a recognized role in society. A family distinguishes you as a "serious person," someone who can take responsibility. That is why in Italy business colleagues will inquire about your family. A family means you have something to lose, a network of support, a sense of responsibility. This gives a sense of belonging that is in no way reflected in modern British or American society.

COMMITMENT

As befits a land with close, long-standing networks of relationships and trust, friends are always in contact with each other. This provides a tremendous sense of security, but for people used to their own space it can all prove rather intense! Your new Italian friends will shower you with invitations so that every weekend there is something to do. The downside is that whenever invited to weddings, birthdays, and funerals, you will be expected to go. The only respite is to leave the country. Unlike the British and the Americans, who, once a connection is made, are able to pick up a conversation several months later, the Italians expect you to maintain constant contact.

The political philosopher Antonio Gramsci wrote: "Rather than joining political parties and trade unions, Italians prefer joining organizations of a different type, like cliques, gangs, *camorras*, and mafias." Circles of friends are just such a clique—supportive, but sometimes a bit stifling.

For an Italian, a relationship implies responsibilities. You don't just drop in or out of a friendship when it pleases you. You are either on the inside or on the outside.

JEALOUSY

June Collins, an attractive single teacher living and working in Italy, discovered another aspect of Italian friendship, based on gender. As Luigi Barzini says in *The Italians*, Italy is a crypto-matriarchy. Men run Italy but women run men. The way they run them is to seduce them. The Italian woman is beautifully turned-out, and, on the surface, quite subservient to men, especially in public. To a young Scot like June, eager to make women friends like those at home in Edinburgh, it was upsetting to find that the other women teachers were wary of her. June was used to holding her own in men's company, and she was surprised to see that Italian women appeared to be more submissive when in a mixed group.

POWER

The secret of any Italian structure, says Barzini, is who holds the power: the ultimate source of power is the family. "Family loyalty," he writes, "is the Italians' true patriotism." This explains why an Italian may behave formally to you in the office but be informal at home. In the home you are part of a different network. Foreigners find the contrast contradictory and even disillusioning. The Italians see no such contradiction. The two worlds are entirely different domains. Any foreign territory is hostile until proven friendly or harmless. If you can't ignore it or adopt it, then you deceive or suborn it in whatever way you can.

INVITATIONS

Invitations home are therefore an important step in the development of a relationship, as are invitations to family events such as birthdays, name-days, weddings, and funerals. If a family invites you to church, do go—even if you aren't Catholic. As the Protestant Henry of Navarre is supposed to have said when invited to be King of France, on condition he converted to Catholicism, "Paris is worth a mass."

GIFT GIVING

Gift giving in some cultures can be a minefield. Common sense will get you through. If invited to an Italian home, gift-wrapped chocolates,

pastries, or flowers are acceptable. Italy is
an "odd number" country, so do not
give an even number of flowers. Also
avoid taking chrysanthemums, which are
laid on graves at funerals and on November 2,
All Souls Day (known as *il Giorno dei Morti*).
Brooches, handkerchiefs, and knives all suggest
sadness or loss so these should be avoided.

SOCIAL CLUBS

Most major Italian cities have expatriate sports
and social clubs and organizations that cater to all
nationalities. The American Women's Club, the
Rotary Club, Anglo-Italian clubs, and Lion Clubs
all have branches in Italy. These can be a real
point of contact for visitors as they offer a wide
range of activities, and short-term membership is
often available. Many organize Italian classes as
well. Clubs are a good way to meet people (check
the local tourist office for details).

BARS AND NIGHTLIFE

On the whole, it's not difficult to meet Italians.
They are outdoorsy and outgoing. Social life
revolves around the piazzas, with their bars and
cafés, many with live music in the evening. There
are even Irish pubs in northern Italy.

For young Italians, there is a lively clubbing culture. Discos are often huge and spread over many floors; they charge a high entrance fee (the price usually includes your first drink). They open around 11:30 p.m. Ask your hotel, or look in the local paper, for the best "in" place of the moment.

If you enjoy gambling and fancy a small wager, you'll need your passport to enter a casino. Italians are not allowed in unless they can prove they are employed. Evening wear is obligatory. Opening hours are from 2:00 or 3:00 p.m. to around 4:30 a.m. Be careful not to confuse the word *casinò* (with the stress on the last syllable), which means casino, with the Italian *casino* (stress on the second syllable), which means brothel!

CONCLUSION

Friendship is a gift and the Italians are famous for it. No people could be warmer or more hospitable, but they realize that friendship must be worked at—it is a contact sport. Regular contact and, where possible, face-to-face meetings, are what count. The building of opportunities to help each other in an inhospitable world is an important part of that. Chapter 5 shows how that belief translates into everyday life.

chapter five

DAILY LIFE

Italian life is rooted in the family and the network of close family friends. As we have seen, they are the ones who can always be relied on. This attitude has led to a realistic and slightly pessimistic view of life.

BIRTH

In Italy the birth of a child is an important event, not just for the family but for the whole neighborhood. Unlike Britain, where traditionally children are "seen but not heard," in Italy children are celebrated. An Italian father's first job is to buy a rosette, blue for a boy, pink for a girl, and stick it the front door. The second is to register the birth within seven days, in the place of birth, and with two witnesses. As we have seen, Italians are born into, live by, and die by bureaucracy.

The Italian birth rate is now the second lowest in Europe, with 1.26 children for every woman of child-bearing age (compared with 1.25 in Spain).

There are signs that from an all-time low of 1.18 children per woman in 1995, it is creeping up in the richer north and central areas of Italy.

EDUCATION

The school year runs from September to June. The state education system is supplemented by private schools, all following the national curriculum. Education starts at an early age: compulsory schooling is from six to fifteen years old, but a child may go to infant school (*scuola dell'infanzia*) as early as four. From six to eleven, children attend primary school (*scuola primaria*). At age eleven, they take the *licenza elementare* before attending middle school (*scuola media*) from eleven to fourteen. At fourteen, they take the *diploma di licenza media*, a year before the end of compulsory schooling.

Between fourteen and eighteen, children have a considerable amount of choice. They might opt for a *liceo classico* (which specializes in a traditional humanistic education), a *liceo scientifico* (scientific studies), a *liceo linguistico* (languages), a *liceo tecnico* (technical studies), or an *istituto commerciale* (commerce). Or they might prefer an arts education in a *liceo artistico*, *istituto d'arte*, *conservatorio* (musical studies), *accademia di danza*, or *accademia drammatica*.

If they want to start teacher training, they will attend an *istituto magistrale* or *scuola magistrale*.

The type of school does not mean that basic subjects are excluded, but that extra hours are devoted to the disciplines in which the school specializes. The *maturità* exam at eighteen allows access to university and the *diploma di laurea* (bachelor's degree).

MILITARY SERVICE AND THE ARMED FORCES

All Italian men are subject to ten months' compulsory military service, though it is due to be phased out in 2005. However, those called up can opt for voluntary service or to work for the Roman Catholic Church instead.

Women can join the armed forces, but they cannot be air force pilots, serve on a submarine, or enlist in the *carabinieri*.

FINDING A JOB

Italy has relatively high unemployment, rising from 8 percent in the North to as high as 21 percent in the South. There are practically no unemployment benefits in Italy and getting on the employment ladder can be hard, even for graduates. Many go from university into vocational courses to learn a trade. One of the main employers is the family firm, where, as we have seen, sons and daughters frequently take over when their father retires. Although Italy has traditionally had the best long-term employment conditions in Europe, more than a quarter of the workforce is now on short-term contracts.

As in Britain, one of the fastest-growing sectors of the Italian economy is the service and leisure industry. On the other hand, a widespread ambition is to become a *statale* (civil servant), which offers security of employment, regular hours, and early retirement on a state pension.

MARRIAGE

Most Italians live at home until they get married. It is not uncommon to find thirty-year-olds still living with their parents, and indeed for married couples to live with parents-in-law while waiting to find a suitable house or apartment to rent or buy. Italian children therefore leave home much later than their British, American, or Australian counterparts.

HOUSING

In the cities, most Italians live in rented apartments, but in the suburbs and small towns

and villages, families own their own houses.
Housing is extremely hard to come by in Italy, and
many people wait years before moving into their
own home. Italian apartments can be quite small.
Three-bedroom apartments are rare
but two bathrooms are common.
The Italians take great pride in
decoration and design and spare
no expense to make their homes
beautiful. The use of marble,
wood, and stone is common. Italy
is famous for its ceramics, which can
be found in bathrooms and in kitchens.
Bathrooms will normally have a toilet and a bidet,
and the washing machine is often placed in the
bathroom rather than the kitchen.

When Italians move they take everything with
them except, literally, the kitchen sink and
perhaps the bath. All furnishings, including
fixtures and fittings, have to be installed, usually
by a local artisan/carpenter. Every Italian has his
or her "special" person whom they will
recommend. Italian floors are usually tiled rather
than carpeted. Parquet flooring is expensive and
tends to be reserved for the "master" bedroom.

One interesting feature of many Italian houses
is the top-floor balcony, which is open to the
elements and called a *loggia*. Another is the
basement *taverna*. This is a sort of playroom or

rumpus room for grownups, which is used for parties and barbecues. It may have a fireplace, wines, rustic-style furniture. Found in newer houses, the *taverna* is a throwback to the old Italian hunting lodge and may be where the *condominio* inhabitants join up with friends on the mid-August bank holiday of *Ferragosto*, or on Liberation Day on April 25.

Some experts say that if you intend to stay in Italy for less than five years it is more economical to rent than to buy, but beyond that it is worth considering buying. Some foreigners buy into a *condominio*, a group of apartments around a garden and perhaps a swimming pool, in which utilities and general upkeep are shared between the owners. If you do this, always make sure that your contract allows you full use of the facilities.

Experts also suggest that, even if you eventually intend to buy, it is better to rent for the first six to nine months, and to do so in the worst part of the year weather-wise. Many foreigners have bought in the balmy spring and autumn and repented at leisure in the steaming hot summer or damp freezing winter.

The Italian rental market is strong, with houses and apartments available in all categories. Rentals are usually unfurnished (*non ammobiliato*), and long-term furnished rentals (*ammobiliato*) are rare. Some properties are rented semi-furnished, in which case they are like a self-catering apartment. For detailed advice on renting or buying accommodation in Italy, consult Graeme Chesters' *Living and Working in Italy* (see Further Reading). One piece of advice he gives is that the worst time to look for apartments or houses is September/October. That is when the Italians are back from vacation and their wanderlust translates into the search for a new home.

SHOPPING

The Italians like to buy their food fresh, and going to the market is an important part of daily life. Italy works on the metric system, and items are bought in kilos (kilograms), half-kilos, or grams (usually measured in hundreds). There are permanent indoor markets, street markets, and traveling markets, which are usually cheaper than stores (depending on your bargaining skills). As well as fresh local produce you can buy all kinds of manufactured products, including clothes.

Supermarkets are not as ubiquitous as in North America or Britain and account for about 6 percent of the Italian food market, as opposed to 50 percent in France. The main chains are Coop, Esselunga, Euromercato, GS, Pam, Standa, and

Unes. Italians take their own bags to the supermarket (plastic bags are usually charged for and there is no "bagging and carry-out" policy).

Milan and Rome are the centers of Italy's department stores, of which the most famous is La Rinascente (www.rinascente.it) as well as Metro, Standa, and Upim. Department stores have international facilities, take credit cards, usually have English speakers, and may well be easier for foreign shoppers than small local stores.

The *saldi* (sales) take place in January, and in July and August before the summer holidays, but even then prices can seem high. (Italian "cheap" is often British or American "expensive.") Sportswear and sports equipment, children's clothing, and toys are also expensive, even in the children's wear chain, Prenatal.

If you are taking children to Italy it is worth making sure you have supplies of their favorite food. It may not be available locally as children's diets in Italy are somewhat different to those in the U.S. and the U.K.

Items that can be hard to find, or are expensive, are electric kettles, duvets, and bayonet light bulbs (only screw-type bulbs are sold in Italy).

Italy works on the standard two-prong round pin at 220 volts and 50 hertz, so although British appliances work perfectly, American ones will need an adaptor. Phone adaptors for modem connection may be different, and you may wish to buy one of the multiadaptor packs available at airport duty-free stores.

Shopping Hours

Shops normally open from about 8:30 a.m. and close around 6:00, 7:00, or 8:00 p.m. Many shops, especially in the South, take a *pausa* (long lunch break) and close between 1:00 p.m. and 3:00 or 4:00 p.m. It is always worth checking opening times. To compensate for Saturday working, many shops close on a weekday afternoon: this varies from city to city. Once again, the advantage of most department stores and supermarkets is that they are open all day.

MONEY AND BANKING

Italy is part of the Eurozone, and since 2002 the lira has no longer been legal tender. There is a strong cash economy, especially outside the major cities. Credit cards may not be accepted everywhere and it is worth checking this in restaurants and shops in smaller towns, and definitely in villages. The strength of the black market in Italy also encourages cash transactions. The important thing is not to rely on one source of funds: take both cash and credit. Always have your passport as ID and be careful of personal security. Travelers' checks are the safest form of currency, but they are not directly cashable in most hotels and restaurants.

ATM outlets, called Bancomats, are available via the CIRRUS and NYCE networks, but they often run out of money or are not in working order, so if you need weekend cash, get there in good time. Most Italian banks don't accept checks drawn on foreign banks, but travelers' checks and foreign currency can be exchanged at banks and at international stations and airports.

It is worth shopping around as rates of exchange can differ markedly. Airports and change machines offer the worst exchange rates and the highest handling charges. Banks offer the best exchange rates and post offices the lowest charges, but to American and British visitors, banks can be quite intimidating, with revolving security doors and armed guards.

Banking hours vary according to the city, but in general are from 8:30 a.m. to 1:30 p.m., and from 2:30 p.m. to 4:00 or 4:30 p.m. In major cities some branches may open from 9:00 a.m. till noon on Saturdays. It is important to check in advance.

Credit Cards

The main credit cards accepted in Italy are Mastercard, Visa, and Carta Sì. Credit cards are less popular than debit cards, but as a foreigner your credit card can be very helpful.

Opening a Bank Account
You will need to open a bank account if you're living in Italy for any length of time. However, it isn't that easy. The majority of banks will only permit foreigners to open an account if they are in possession of a residence certificate (*certificato di residenza*). It might make life easier if you approached an Italian bank with overseas branches (*filiali*), like the Banca di Roma, before departure. Other people feel the personal approach works best, so when in Italy, try to go with a friend who is known to the bank.

To open an account as a foreigner, you'll need the following:
• Valid passport
• Valid residence certificate
• Proof of address in Italy, e.g. telephone or electricity bill, rental contract

Other useful facts about Italian banking are that bounced checks are illegal, overdrafts are very expensive, postdating checks is also illegal, and checks can be cleared on the day of writing regardless of the date. You can only stop a check if it has been lost or stolen, in which case you must report it to the police or the *carabinieri.*

KEEPING HEALTHY

A recent survey showed that Italians are among the healthiest and longest-lived people in Europe—due, it is said, to red wine, olive oil, and a Mediterranean diet. According to UN figures, men tend to live to seventy-six and women to eighty-two.

Italian health care expenditure is low, about 6 percent of GDP, and the standard of hospitals, especially in the South, varies widely. However, Italian doctors and medical staff are among the best-trained in the world, and Italy has the highest number of doctors per capita of any country (1 per 160 inhabitants). Many speak English. There is also a medical service for tourists with English-speaking staff (*guardia medica turistica*), and it is worth asking your embassy or consulate for a list of local English-speaking doctors.

Although Italy has a national health service (the *servizio sanitario nazionale,* or SSN, established in 1978), some Italians buy private health insurance. If you are living in Italy for any length of time, it is worth your doing so too. For Britons, who are members of the EU, an E111 form from the local British post office confirms your right to low-cost or free medical treatment on the Italian national health service, which provides free emergency health care to visitors, regardless of nationality.

If you are ill you can attend a family doctor (*medico generico*) or a health clinic (*azienda sanità locale*, or ASL) or you can go to the emergency department (*pronto soccorso*) of the local hospital (*ospedale*). Hospitals are marked with a white H on a blue background. Make sure you have the relevant insurance card as you will be required to pay before you receive treatment. If you are in Rome, try the Salvator Mundi International Hospital or the Rome American Hospital, or in Milan, the Milan Clinic, where English-speaking staff are available.

If a local doctor prescribes medicine for you, it will be dispensed in a *farmacia*. Note that the word *droga* is reserved exclusively for narcotics. Homeopathic medicines are popular in Italy and are often prescribed by doctors and stocked by all chemists. You will normally see a green sign, saying *Omeopatia*.

Always get your teeth attended to before you go to Italy. There are few dentists per capita, fewer still speak English, and charges are very high. Although it is possible to be seen by an optician on the national health service in Italy, it is simpler to get things checked before you go. Remember to take a spare pair of glasses with you and a copy of your eyeglasses prescription in case of emergency.

Other items that you might expect to find at a chemist or pharmacy in Britain or the States are sold in general stores or boutiques. Pharmacies in Italy are reserved for medicine. For natural toiletries and cosmetics, one British store that is well represented in Italy is the Bodyshop.

If you need more supplies of a regular medicine, take a packet with you as, although the brand may be different, the pharmacist will be able to recognize the ingredients. Italian pharmacists often have the knowledge and authority to advise on a wider range of medicine and treatments for ailments than may be the case in the U.K.

Spas

One of the pleasures of Italy is the *terme*, or spas, offering not just immersion in spa waters but hydrotherapy and beauty treatments. Health care tourism is big business in Italy, and millions of Italians go to the country's more than one hundred spas every year. Spas can be found in the north near Milan, in Tuscany (Montecatini is one of the most famous), and also on the island of Ischia in the south. Costs are not excessive and it is a pleasant way to detox and chill out.

TIME OUT

EATING AND DRINKING

One of the great pleasures of Italy is eating and drinking. Each region has its individual cooking style and ingredients. In the north black pepper, butter, and rice are the staples. In the south it's hot red pepper, olive oil, and pasta. In Piedmont scented truffle may be grated over your risotto, Liguria has a pasta sauce of crushed basil and pine nuts called *pesto*, in Tuscany you may eat fresh-caught hare and tomato, or wild-boar sausages, and in Sicily you will be offered the most delicious sardines. Many of these ingredients will have been prepared that day, bought fresh from the market.

Italy's rich diversity and localism explains why there are over two thousand names for the huge variety of pasta shapes, and more wine labels—at least four thousand—than anywhere else in the world. Italy has many food festivals, called *sagre*, where local food is on display for tasting. Wine and truffle festivals are very popular. The Italian state tourist office, ENIT, publishes a booklet on the local festivals called *An Italian Year*.

Meal Culture

In Italy breakfast (*prima colazione*) is normally around 8:00 a.m. and consists of biscuits or croissants, accompanied by strong coffee or perhaps tea. The main meal of the day is often lunch (*pranzo*), which starts anywhere between 1:00 and 2:00 p.m. and may last up to three hours (depending on the region), although office workers will usually eat and leave faster. If a heavy lunch has been eaten, the evening meal may consist of a light snack.

Dinner (*cena*) is usually around 8:00 p.m., but may be as late as 10:00 p.m. If the breadwinner cannot get back for lunch, dinner becomes the main meal. Children tend to stay up late, with no fixed bedtimes. Bread without butter is served and there is usually wine and water. When the family has guests, the head of the household pours the first round of wine and may propose a toast (*brindisi*) and then everyone serves themselves. "Cheers" in Italian is "*Salute.*"

A full-scale Italian meal is substantial, and so varied that it bears out the adage, *l'appetito vien mangiando* (the appetite grows with eating). Two main courses are preceded by a starter and followed by cheese, a dessert, and/or fruit. The starter, or *antipasto*, is often a selection of cold meats and marinated vegetables. Parma ham and melon are popular *antipasti*.

The first main dish, the *primo*, is usually pasta or risotto or perhaps a soup (*minestra*). *Minestrone* is a vegetable soup. The second main course, or *secondo*, will be meat or fish plus a cooked vegetable, often served separately as a side dish (*contorno*). The *contorni* (including potatoes) often follow the second dish as they are seen as palette cleansers rather than as an accompaniment to the meat or fish. Pasta is almost never eaten as a meal in itself, except for lasagne, and if you feel a whole portion of pasta as a first course is too much for you, it is acceptable to ask for a *mezza porzione* (half portion).

This may be followed by cheese and fruit, then dessert (*dolce*) and coffee. It is absolutely normal for Italians to drink wine with their meal, even in working hours. Tap water (*acqua semplice*) is free, but most Italians will ask for mineral water (*acqua minerale*), either sparkling (*gassata*) or still (*non-gassata*).

The bill (*conto*) will include Value Added Tax (IVA in Italian), and either a cover charge for *pane e coperto* ("bread and cover") or a service charge (*servizio*) of around 12 percent. This does not go to your waiter so you may wish to add an extra few euros for him or her. Because of the prevalence of tax evasion in Italy, all shops, restaurants, and bars are required by law to issue customers with a *scontrino* (receipt). If they do not do so, they can be fined heavily.

Tipping is entirely at your discretion. Many restaurants have a service charge. The Italians are not generous tippers. If tipping for good service, they generally round up the bill to the nearest euro. A small gratuity is normally left for hotel porters and doormen and also chambermaids. Taxi fares may be rounded up, and if you buy a drink at the bar a small coin for the barman is often left along with the tab for your drink.

A TIME TO RELAX
No one is in a hurry when eating out in Italy. The interval between the *secondo piatto* and the cheese and fruit, followed by dessert and coffee, is the time for leisurely conversation and may easily add an hour to your meal.

Italians eat out a great deal and there is a wide range of establishments, all clearly identified. A *ristorante* (restaurant) is usually the most expensive option. A *trattoria* is a small local restaurant, usually family-run and mid-priced, offering a limited menu, but sometimes with excellent food. A *taverna* or *osteria* is simpler and

less pretentious. However, always check the menu
first as the type of restaurant isn't always an
indication of price.

Italians tend not to frequent burger joints,
unless they have children. A pizzeria with a wood-
burning stove is very popular, as is a *gelateria*, or
ice-cream parlor. For quick meals, a *rosticceria*
does spit-roasted meats and precooked chicken
dishes. A *tavola calda* is a modest hot food bar. An
enoteca (wine shop) may serve basic meals to
accompany the usually excellent wines. Look for
signs saying "*Cucina casalinga*": this means the
food is home-cooked, simple, unfussy, but
satisfying. Avoid the *menu turistico* or *menu a
prezzo fisso* (set-price meal) unless you want to eat
quickly and cheaply, as the standard is often poor.

Drinking

In Italy it is common to drink an *aperitivo*

(aperitif) before meals. This may be a light
white wine such as a Verdicchio or a
Prosecco. Or you may be offered a
spumante (sparkling wine). White and
red wine (*vino bianco* and *vino rosso*)
will be served during the meal. Wine
can be ordered by the carafe (*caraffa*),
quarter-liter (*quartino*), half-liter
(*mezzo litro*), or liter (*litro*). Most Italians
opt for the house wine (*vino della casa*), usually

red. The meal may be followed by a *digestivo* (digestive), such as a cognac, a *grappa* (Italian brandy), or an *amaro* (a vermouth-type liqueur).

Like many Latins, Italians are not heavy drinkers and prefer to drink with food. Monsignor Della Casa in the *Galateo*, a manual of etiquette published in 1555, writes, "I thank God that for all the many other plagues that have come to us from beyond the Alps, this most pernicious custom of making game of drunkenness, and even admiring it, has not reached as far as this."

Stand or Sit?

If you are in a hurry and just want a quick coffee, or a refreshing drink, go into a bar and drink standing up at the counter (*al banco*). It is up to three times cheaper than sitting at a table inside or out on the terrace. Why? Because when you sit down, you have paid not just for a drink but for a "pitch" where you can talk, write, read, or watch the world go by. There will be no pressure to move on, although the waiter will ask if he/she can get you another drink.

Although Italian alcohol consumption is among the highest in Europe, it is spread evenly across the population and most people probably drink little more than a couple of glasses of wine a day. The idea of drinking to get drunk is foreign to the Italians. They may have a glass of *grappa* with their morning coffee, but alcohol is really seen as an accompaniment to food.

Beer Culture

Although Italy is famous for its wines, beer is also popular. Moretti, Frost, and Peroni are popular local brands, served *alla spina* (draught), *piccola* (20 cl), *media* (40 cl), and *grande* (66 cl). For soft drinks, try *granita*, an iced summer drink made with lemon, orange, mint, strawberry, or coffee.

Coffee and Tea

Few people in Britain or North America need educating about Italian coffee culture. Listed below are the most frequently ordered types. (Note that if you ask for *un caffè*, this means a small black *espresso*.)

Coffee

Espresso: small strong black coffee (*doppio espresso* is double-size).

Caffè lungo: small and black, but weaker than *espresso*.

Caffè corretto: black with a shot of *grappa* (or some other liqueur).

Caffè macchiato: black with a dash of milk.

Caffelatte: a large coffee with lots of milk.

Cappuccino: coffee with a thick layer of frothy milk and a scattering of chocolate on top (only drunk by Italians with breakfast and up to mid-morning).

If you want a decaffeinated coffee, ask for *un decaffeinato* or *un caffè Hag*. This isn't drunk much in Italy. If you ask for tea, you will be brought hot water with a tea bag . By law, Italian bars and cafés must serve you a glass of water free of charge regardless of whether you buy anything.

DRESS

Italy is an extremely fashion-conscious culture, and Italian women, in particular, expect to spend a large percentage of their disposable income on clothes and accessories. You are how you dress, and clothes are a badge of success. Women wear quiet, well-cut, expensive and elegant clothes, and men's ties and suits should also be fashionable and well-tailored. Even casual clothes are smart and chic. Remember that Italy, especially Milan, is a center of European fashion. Dress codes are relaxed, but Italian women do not normally wear shorts in the cities. In churches, as we have seen, you may be forbidden to enter if you are wearing shorts or a sleeveless top.

OUTDOOR LIFE

One of the great delights of Italy is how much of life is lived outdoors, at least in the warmer months of the year. All large towns have more or less permanent outdoor markets and every village has a lively market day.

Sunday at the beach is a family ritual. After hours of preparation, the family emerges in public on the beach, the mother leading her flock to the chosen spot. As Tim Parks commented, in Italy, despite its individualism, people tend to do the same thing at the same time, whether it be tending a grave or going to the beach on June 18 after schools let out.

A characteristic of Southern life in particular is the *passeggiata*, a ritual more unmissable than Sunday mass. Young people gather in the hour or so before dinner and whole families put on their best clothes and walk arm-in-arm through the streets to see and be seen.

The Italians also enjoy camping, and Italy has over two thousand campsites, mostly open from April through September. They are graded according to facilities, from one to four stars; the best may have their own supermarkets, swimming pools, and cinemas. You may need an international camping ticket book: this can usually be bought at the campsite.

Tip for Campers
If you're heading for a campsite, aim to arrive by
11:00 a.m. If you wait until after lunch, all the
spaces may have gone.

FOOTBALL AS A WAY OF LIFE

Some observers have called football (soccer)
Italy's real religion. In Italy football is an art
and is described as such by commentators
and spectators alike. Watching the local team
on a Sunday is an important event, and a
national team's success will be celebrated in
banner headlines. The top teams such as
Juventus (Turin), AC Milan, Inter Milan,
and Lazio (Rome) are owned by leading business
and political figures and are as much symbols of
Italian pride as Benetton, Ferrari, Fiat, Armani,
or Versace.

With the verbal felicity for which Italians are
famed, footballers are given nicknames. Marco
van Basten is called "the swan," for example, and
the Brazilian, Cafu, is "the little pendulum."

In some ways, the rivalry between Italian clubs
reflects the ancient rivalry between the medieval
city-states; the drama is played out in stadiums
across the country every week in season. Sit in
any café (called *bar* in Italian) with its big screen

and enjoy the exhilaration when the home team scores and share the misery when they lose a match. Strategy and tactics are discussed endlessly and with passion.

SEEING THE SIGHTS

There is so much for the visitor to see in Italy, but where to start? A good idea is to visit the local office of the national tourist board, ENIT (*Ente Nazionale Italiano di Turismo*). They have offices in London and New York as well as at most of Italy's border posts and airports. The state travel agency, CIT or CIT Italia (*Sestante-Compagnia Italiana di Turismo*), also provides information, and has a train-booking service. Each of Italy's twenty provincial capitals has a local tourist office, called EPT (*Ente Provinciale di Turismo*) or APT (*Azienda di Promozione Turistica*). IAT (*Ufficio Informazione e Accoglienza Turistica*) and AAST (*Azienda Autonoma di Soggiorno e Turismo*) all provide maps, local information, public transport details, and opening times of the main sights in the area. Opening times are usually 8:30 a.m. to 7:00 p.m., Monday to Friday.

A National Call Center for English-speaking tourists is available on 800-117 700. It provides information in English on health care, safety, museums, accommodation, events, and shows.

FESTIVALS

As we have seen, the annual *festa* in an Italian
town is an important event and can last several
days. It may be a religious celebration, and it may
also date back to Renaissance or medieval times:
examples are the *Palio* horseback races in Siena
(July 2 and August 16), the *Regata* in Venice (the
first Sunday in September), and the *Scoppio del
Carro* ("Firing of the Cart") at Easter in Florence.
On three days in June, one of which is always June
24, Florence is the venue for the sixteenth-century
costume parade (*Calcio Storico Fiorentino*). There
is also the lively sweet and toy fair from Christmas
to January 5 in Rome's Piazza Navona.

MUSEUMS AND ART GALLERIES

There are some seventy state-run museums in
Italy, and one estimate says that the country is
home to half the world's great art treasures. Part
of the reason is the extraordinary flowering of art
and sculpture in Renaissance Italy, the legacy of
which is visible in churches, palaces, and
museums throughout the land. Almost every
church seems to have its masterpiece—and almost
every church wants to charge you 3 euros to enter
and find it! Museums often close on Mondays, to
compensate for being open on the weekend, and
are usually open Tuesday through Saturday from

9:00 a.m. to 1:00 or 2:00 p.m. (later in big cities), and on Sundays from 9:00 a.m. to 1:00 p.m.

Some of the sites are so famous that you might think they are overrated: don't be put off! The lines in the Vatican City may try your patience, but the soaring roof of the Sistine Chapel, once you squeeze through its narrow door, is breathtaking. The Villa Borghese in Rome is a gem, as are the Accademia and the Peggy Guggenheim Museum of Modern Art in Venice, and the Uffizi in Florence. Although Venice, Florence, and Rome draw the crowds, it is well worth visiting Naples, Palermo, and smaller towns such as Padua, Siena, and Pisa.

Some galleries such as the Villa Borghese require prior booking. Churches have a dress code. No bare shoulders or shorts, and visitors are asked not to wander around when a service is in progress.

MONUMENTS

Some of the best-preserved monuments of ancient Greek civilization are found in southern Italy, known as Magna Graecia (Greater Greece) when it was a Greek colony. The most impressive temples are at Paestum (south of Naples), and at Selinunte, Agrigento, and Segesta in Sicily. The theater at Syracuse is the largest in the world.

One of the most memorable ways to gain a

sense of Italy's multilayered civilizations is to visit the church of San Clemente in Rome, overseen by Irish Dominicans. The eleventh-century upper church contains a magnificent Romanesque mosaic, but also Renaissance wall paintings and lavish Baroque decor. Under its floor you can visit a fourth-century church containing fragments of frescos, one of them with the oldest description in Italian. Descending even further, some 100 feet (30 meters) below street level, you find yourself in a narrow alley in ancient Rome leading to a first-century patrician house and a Mithraic temple.

For the glory that was Roman Italy, you must go to Pompeii and Herculaneum (Ercolano). Both were buried by the volcanic eruption of Mount Vesuvius, in 79 CE, and the site was not excavated until 1750. And, yes, if you're in Naples, it's worth the trip. Pompeii is open from 8:00 a.m. to 7:30 p.m., Monday through Saturdays, and you need three or four hours to take it all in.

MUSIC AND THEATER

The country of Verdi and Puccini is not short of opera houses and theaters. Italy hosts many world-renowned opera performances, and, if you speak Italian, you can see plays by names such as Pirandello and Dario Fo. The opera season runs from December to June, but there are summer

festivals in open-air theaters. One of the greatest outdoor concert venues is Verona's huge first-century amphitheater, known as the "Arena," which can seat an audience of up to 25,000. Large as it is, the Arena is dwarfed by Rome's

Colosseum, which, in its day, could hold 50,000 spectators. The most famous opera is La Scala in Milan; you can book ahead on www.musica.it.

If you stroll around the piazza in front of the Doge's Palace in Venice, sellers in eighteenth-century costume will give you fliers for baroque music in the Venetian style, performed in concert halls in the center of the city. Tourist trap though it may be, the music is usually enjoyable and respectably played. You'll enjoy your late evening *grappa* in the famous Caffè Florian even more.

Music festivals are also popular in Italy. One of the most famous is the Festival of Two Worlds in

Spoleto in June and July. The Sanremo Italian popular song festival (Festival della Canzone Italiana) in February is the equivalent of the Grammy or the Brit awards.

Apart from open-air festivals, all the opera houses and theaters, as well as the majority of cinemas, shut their doors in the summer. Entertainment moves outside with feasting, dancing, and music in the courtyards of old palazzos, and opera in city parks and amphitheaters. This is also the season for a thousand local *festas*, or festivals.

CINEMA

In Italy, almost all foreign films are dubbed. Italian cinema has a great tradition, however. Fellini's old home in Via Marghera in Rome has a commemorative plaque outside, and Rome's Cinecittà film studios were home to Sergio Leone's "spaghetti westerns," which made Clint Eastwood famous. In the major cities you will find at least one cinema showing English-language films in the original. The Venice Film Festival in August and September is the world's oldest film festival (founded in 1932) and a major event in the international calendar. Venice's Golden Lion is one of international cinema's most prestigious awards.

chapter seven

GETTING AROUND

"Who has been to Italy," proclaimed the Russian author Nicolai Gogol to his friend Zhukovsky, "can forget all other regions…Europe compared to Italy is like a gloomy day compared to a day of sunshine." Admiring Italy is one thing. Getting around it may be another matter.

In the eighteenth century, when traveling around Europe on the "Grand Tour" was *de rigueur* for young noblemen, Italy was where they learned to become "perfect gentlemen." A trip to Venice, Florence, Rome, and Naples was an essential part of a man's education. The compiler of Britain's first English dictionary, Dr. Samuel Johnson, wrote, "A man who has not been to Italy is always conscious of an inferiority, for his not having seen what a man is expected to see."

So much for what to see. What about how to get there? The good news is that things have improved since the days of the Grand Tour. Brigands no longer haunt the mountain passes, and the advice given to tourists by Murray's *Guide to Southern Italy* in 1858 to " . . . make their bargains with the landlords on their first arrival," is no longer necessary. However, all of Italy's transport systems, like Britain's, can be uncertain and the great quality you need—as always in Italy—is a degree of flexibility.

AIR TRAVEL AND ENTRY TO ITALY

Since Italy is a member of the European Union and the Eurozone, any EU citizen can enter freely. North Americans need a passport, but not a visa.

The main points of entry are Rome's Leonardo da Vinci (also known as Fiumicino) and Ciampino airports, and Milan's Malpensa and Linate airports.

Alitalia and ATI are the Italian international and domestic carriers. The best way to book an internal flight is through a recognized travel agency, and a wide range of discounted fares are available on both national and international flights. (It's important to ask for these discounts; they are rarely offered automatically.) To contact Alitalia or ATI by Internet, go to www.alitalia.it.

POLICE REGISTRATION

By law, non-EU visitors staying more than three days in Italy are required to register with the police. A hotel will do this for you automatically, but if you are staying with friends you need to go to the local *Questura*, or *Commissariato*, or *Stazione dei Carabinieri*. Because, as we have seen, Italy can be extremely bureaucratic, it is worth taking an Italian friend with you to see that everything goes smoothly.

If you are a non-EU citizen and are staying for longer than ninety days, you need to get a *permesso di soggiorno* (residence permit) within eight days of arrival. These are issued by the *Ufficio Stranieri* (foreign department) or *Questura* of the police, and you need an official letter stamped with the *bollo* (state stamp).

THE UBIQUITOUS *BOLLO*

An important part of anyone's life in Italy is the *bollo*, a special type of state postage stamp, affixed to official documents and requests, which attests that the relevant administration fee has been paid. *Bolli*  are sold at *tabacchi* (tobacco kiosks), as indeed is the special legal paper on which you must write your formal request. This is called *carta uso bollo*, or *carta bollata*.

The complexity and time-wasting of much of Italy's bureaucracy has led to the creation of large numbers of agencies (*agenzie*) that specialize in getting your documents for you, obtaining the necessary stamps, and standing in the inevitable lines. Many people find the convenience and expertise of this service worth the extra cost.

RESIDENCY

Where an *agenzia* may seem a blessing is in getting a residency certificate (*certificato di residenza*) and a tax code (*codice fiscale*). If you are settling in Italy for any length of time, the *certificato di residenza* is essential: you will need it when buying a car or when getting utilities such as gas and the phone connected. The *codice fiscale* is useful as an ID, and may be demanded for anything such as joining a club or opening a bank account.

To get a *certificato di residenza*, take your *permesso di soggiorno* and your ID to the *Ufficio Anagrafe* and apply to be registered with the local *comune*. Buy some *bolli* and take them with you so that the official can affix them to the document.

For the *codice fiscale*, you take your passport and ID card to the provincial tax office, the *Ufficio Imposte Dirette*, which will issue the card.

With the number of documents the average Italian has to carry, is it any wonder that Italy pioneered the fashion handbag for men?

PUBLIC AND PRIVATE TRANSPORT

Italy's public transport system is reasonably priced by European standards, but chaotic because it is plagued by strikes. Italy has both a public and a private transport system. The latter operates on a local basis in towns and outlying villages. The train system is mainly state-owned and can be inefficient, unpunctual, and strike-ridden, although the modern trains are extremely comfortable.

Trains

The state railway is called the *ferrovia statale*. The timetable is available on www.trenitalia.com.

Nonresidents can buy an Italy Rail Card, which gives unlimited travel for up to thirty days. There is also an Italy Flexi-card for four, eight, or twelve days up to one month. This is available from ticket offices at railway stations and from travel agencies.

There is a range of different types of train service, all with different prices.

The ETR 450 Pendolino is a first-class high-speed train, equivalent to France's TGV. These run mainly from the southern region of Puglia, through Rome to Milan, and seats need to be reserved in advance. The Eurostar (Italia), like the Pendolino, needs advance reservation. The *espresso* and the *diretto* cover local distances but stop at main stations only. The *locale* is the slow local train, which stops for long periods at stations—fun to travel on if you have the time.

There is a huge range of discounts and special tickets and it is worth asking at a booking agency what is available. If you buy your ticket on the train, there is a surcharge of 20 percent, and if reserved seats are not occupied as the train leaves, other passengers have the right to occupy them. One important point: you must "validate" your ticket before you travel by punching it into a machine on the platform: if you fail to do so, you will be charged a hefty fine.

The *Metropolitana*

Milan, Genoa, Rome, Naples, and Palermo all have subway systems, although the network does not cover the whole city. Transport is cheap and there is usually an overall flat fee for bus or tram. Since the ticket is valid for more than an hour (e.g. seventy-five minutes in Milan and Rome, ninety minutes in Genoa), it can be used for more than one journey. Except in Rome, this also applies to transfers between bus and metro.

Tickets can be confusing. Metro stations have no ticket offices, and so tickets must be bought at newsstands along main routes or near the metro stations. Look for a big sign that says T for *tabacchi* (tobacconist). Tickets can be bought singly or in a book of ten. Day and weekly tickets are also available.

Buses and Coaches

You should get on a bus or tram at the back, through the doors marked *Salita* (entry). The middle doors are used for getting off, and are marked *Uscita* (exit). Validate your ticket by pressing it into the yellow or orange machine just inside the door. Don't automatically expect a seat. Buses and trams are crowded and children do not normally get up if an adult is standing. Watch out for pickpockets in a crowd and be prepared to shout "*Permesso!*" (Excuse me) or "*Scendo!*" (I'm getting off!) when you reach your stop.

Coach services between cities are popular and inexpensive. Coach companies also offer guided tours, including several major cities. For example, it is possible to do Venice, Padua, and Florence in one day or, in the South, Rome, Naples, Pompeii, and Sorrento. Round the City tours are a good way of getting to know the lay of the land when you have just arrived; they are a little like the Gray Line tours of American cities.

Taxis

Travel by taxi is common in Italy, but you can't usually flag one down in the street. There are taxi stands in piazzas and at stations, but the best way is to phone from a hotel, restaurant, or bar. Fares are shown on the meter, but there is an extra charge if you have luggage, are traveling after 10:00 p.m. on Sundays or public holidays, or are taking a long-distance trip out of town or to an airport. If you want to tip, round up the fare to the nearest euro.

Standing in Line

This is not an Italian custom. Be prepared to use your elbows a bit or be carried along with the crowd, particularly in the South. Until the recent introduction of a numbered waiting system, in most public buildings one would have to try to catch the employee's eye. He or she would decide whom to serve first. Even today, a degree of assertiveness is necessary.

Driving

And so we come to cars. Italian traffic is a nightmare. People drive fast, and park in very narrow spaces with little regard for other cars, animals, or pedestrians. Pedestrian crossings are rarely respected, and an Italian saying goes that "Red traffic lights are only a suggestion!" Added to which, the confusion of cars, buses, and mopeds all jostle through narrow city streets. To walk around Rome's *centro storico* (historic center), where cars cannot easily get through, is a pleasure, and Venice is traffic-free bliss. Other places  where motorists must leave their cars outside the city limits are the hill towns of Umbria and Tuscany, and of course Venice itself. Even though all towns now have traffic-free zones in their historic centers, this increases congestion outside.

Drivers entering Italy from the relative peace of France and Switzerland can be dazed by the intensity and apparent chaos of the traffic. Italy has the second-highest percentage of car ownership in the world after the U.S.A. and since most people live in high-rise buildings their parked cars block the roads and pavements. *Automobile* (with the stress on the third syllable) is the word for car in Italian, but most Italians say *mácchina* (stress on the first syllable; the machine).

Florence and Naples are two of the worst cities for traffic congestion. Fortunately, if you need to get around by other means than on foot, there are alternatives.

Rent a Scooter

That's what the natives do, and not just the young ones. You don't need a driver's license for a *motorino*, and although the law demands a crash helmet, many spurn it as a degrading curb on their freedom. Scooter drivers often go around the city in packs.

Rent a Bike

Dangerous in the big towns, but cycling is a popular weekend sport. The place to do this is in the flat lands of the lower Po Valley, in quiet provincial towns like Mantua or Ferrara.

Rent a Car

There are car-rental offices at major stations and airports. The regulations stipulate that you must be at least nineteen years old, and there is actually a law that says that unless you have held a license for more than three years you cannot drive a car with more than 93 mph (150 kph) speed capacity.

Driving a Car

Italians may be fast and rule-breaking but they are quite safety conscious. They are often excellent drivers, and the Italian accident rate is by no means the highest in Europe. Italian drivers may be assertive, but they are also careful not to damage their paintwork. They do, however, ignore

speed limits unless they spot a speed control or a
motor cycle policeman. "Me first" is the rule, and
over-courteous foreign drivers can actually
cause accidents.

Expressways: 130 kph (81 mph)	
Urban stretches: 90 kph (55 mph)	
Dual highways: 110 kph (68 mph)	
Outside built-up areas: 110 kph (68 mph)	
Built-up areas: 50 kph (30 mph)	

The *carabinieri* (police) and *polizia stradale*
(traffic police) can give you an on-the-spot fine
for speeding, and will also fine you for not having
your traffic documents or internationally required
equipment such as a fluorescent life jacket or red
warning triangle in case of breakdown. The police
may ask for your *patente* (driver's license), *libretto*
(registration document/logbook), *assicurazione*
(insurance), and *carta verde* (green card). It is
worth obtaining an international driver's license
before you leave home as it will facilitate matters
if you get into trouble.

rental supply?

Gasoline (Benzina)
Two types are available, leaded (*piombo*) and
unleaded (*verde*—green). Except on expressways,
service stations tend to keep to shop hours (see

8:30 AM - 6, 7 or 8 PM

Chapter 5, Daily Life) and to close on Sundays. To plug the gap, self-service pumps are available in larger towns. Most gas stations are not automated, but tipping the attendant is not expected. Diesel pumps are marked *gasolio*.

Breakdown

In this case, you need the *autosoccorso* (breakdown service) and *autoservizio* (repairs garage). Telephone the ACI (*Automobile Club d'Italia*) for help. The emergency number for police, doctor or ambulance is 113.

↳ dial 116

Parking

It has been estimated that an Italian motorist spends seven years of his or her life in a car, two of them looking for a parking space. In cities it is best to park wherever you can and proceed on foot or by public transport. A tow-away zone is marked by pictures and the legend *Zona Rimozione* or *Rimozione forzata*. Reclaiming your car is expensive.

Be careful if you park in a street: if it is scheduled for cleaning that night, and your car is causing an obstruction, it will be towed away. Avoid parking where there are no other cars: other people may know something you don't. Streets are cleaned once a week, and every street affected has a sign giving the dates and times.

Finally, a parked car is an invitation to thieves. Never leave anything visible inside your car.

Common Italian Roadsigns	
Pericolo	Danger
Alt/ Avanti	Stop/Go
Entrata/Uscita	Entry/Exit
Rallentare	Slow down
Senso unico	One way
Deviazione	Deviation
Lavori in corso	Roadworks
Limite di velocità	Speed limit
Divieto di sorpasso	No passing
Divieto di sosta	No parking
Parcheggio	Parking

Expressways
There are over 3,700 miles (6,000 km) of expressways in Italy, most of them toll roads. A green sign with a white A marks the *autostrada*, followed by the number. You take a ticket as you enter and pay as you leave. If you want to pay by card, a *Viacard* or *Telepass* is available from toll booths and expressway services.

Autoclubs
The Italian automobile club is called *Automobile Club d'Italia* (ACI). It offers a breakdown service that can be accessed by dialing 116.

Road Rules

Driving is on the right, and you give way to traffic from the right at traffic circles and crossroads. You are required by law to have a warning triangle in the trunk of your car and to carry your road documents (license and car registration) at all times. It is also necessary to have a basic first-aid package and spare warning lights. *(flourescent triangle? p.120*

Traffic crossings are often ignored, but the police will fine you on the spot if a child between the ages of four and twelve is not wearing a seat belt. Children under four must be in a child safety seat, or an on-the-spot fine will be issued. Drivers commonly plead innocence in an attempt to reduce the amount; if you can't pay immediately, you have a sixty-day grace period.

Buying a Car

To buy a car you need your *codice fiscale,* and to be registered as a local resident. To complete the transactions, you accompany the seller to the local ACI (*Automobile Club d'Italia*). The transfer of ownership is known as a *trapasso.* Your primary car operating costs are insurance and road tax. An MOT (called *revisione*) is necessary for cars over three years old, and every two years afterward. They receive a *bollino blu* to show they are clean.

Driving Your Own Car in Italy
Within the EU, foreigners can drive their own car for up to twelve months. British-registered cars with GB plates can only be driven for up to six months. It may be cheaper and less time-consuming to buy a car locally. Importing your own vehicle is both expensive and complicated.

Licenses
If you have an EU driving license you can use it in Italy for an unlimited period. If you decide to live in Italy, you can still use your EU license but you must get it stamped at your local motor registry or ACI office to show you are resident. If you have a larger vehicle than Class B, then you need to reapply for an Italian license.

If you are a non-EU citizen you can drive for up to a year on your driver's license (although you should have a translation into Italian). However, to avoid taking an Italian driving test, you must apply for the Italian license before the year is up or before you get a residence permit.

Many international drivers buy an international driver's license every year rather than go through the process of getting an Italian driver's license, which can be lengthy and time-consuming. Driver's licenses are obtained through the *comune* or *municipio* (town hall). Armed with an Italian translation of your driver's license, you fill in a special form on *carta uso bollo* with the appropriate number of *bolli*. This needs to be stamped at the *pretura* (magistrate's court) and taken to the *comune* with three passport-size photos. One of your photos should be authenticated by the *comune*.

You also need a *certificato medico* (medical certificate). This starts with a medical report form and a blank medical certificate. The medical report is signed by your family doctor; and the certificate, plus *bollo*, plus photo, is taken to the *unità sanitaria locale* (USL) for an eye test and a signature on the certificate.

All this finally goes to the local *motorizazzione civile* with your driver's license, a photocopy of it, and a postal order and another *bollo*. In all, you will need to obtain five documents to acquire an Italian driver's license. Thankfully, today everything can be done through the ACI.

Ferries
Some of the glories of Italy are its islands and lakes. There are some 4,650 miles (7,500 km) of coastline and the ferry services are good. Two of the most popular excursions are from

Naples to Capri and Ischia. Naples to Sicily by hydrofoil (*aliscafo*) is five and a half hours.

chapter eight

BUSINESS BRIEFING

Italy's manufacturers, middlemen, and entrepreneurs are very able producers, promoters, and salespeople, and experienced at thinking internationally. "*Il made in Italy*" is a mark of

high-quality design and function in fashion, in cars, in food and drink, and in white goods. The "Economic Miracle" of the 1950s transformed much of Italian business, in particular the go-ahead family firm.

By the end of the 1980s, Italy claimed to be the fifth-largest economy in the world after Germany, France, Japan, and the U.S.A. However, it may be bigger—an estimated one third of the economy is dominated by what is called the black or "gray" economy, unreported in statistics or tax returns.

BUSINESS IN ITALY

The three sectors of the Italian economy are the state, the conglomerates, and small- and medium-sized enterprises.

The State Sector

The Italian government still has a strong indirect role in business, despite the privatization of public corporations over the last twenty years, and government spending as a proportion of GDP is the highest in the EU. One in five employees works for the public sector, which accounts for the majority of business funding.

Privately Owned Conglomerates

The private sector is dominated by a small number of key families that control major industries and have cross-interests—Berlusconi, Agnelli, Pirelli, De Benedetti (the *salotto buono*). Their conglomerates include international household names such as Fiat, Benetton, Versace, Armani, and Olivetti. These are large corporations but, with the retirement and death of their founders, their interests are diminishing, and new companies with professional management, such as Bulgari, are following in their footsteps.

Small Business

The majority of businesses, especially in the North, are small- and medium-sized family-owned firms, in which the son or daughter takes over on the retirement of the father. Their productivity is higher than in the state sector. They tend to pay cash, employ family and friends, and outsource work to avoid banks, unions, and taxes. These enterprises now face stiff competition from the conglomerates, both national and international, with their higher output, lower costs, and resources to spend on technological innovation. Other obstacles to competitiveness are low investment in research and development and the inefficiency of public institutions. Ninety percent of all Italian companies are SMGs with fewer than fifteen employees.

The *Mezzogiorno* (South) begins just south of Rome (some say it includes Rome!). Northerners are widely seen as more interested in money, Southerners as more concerned with power and the good life. Unemployment is 5 percent in the North and 22 percent in the South. Northerners criticize Southerners for grabbing state subsidies and handouts. The Southerners criticize the Northerners for exploiting labor and diverting savings into their factories.

COMPANY STRUCTURE AND ORGANIZATION

An Italian company is managed by a board of directors (*consiglio d'amministrazione*) under a president (*presidente*). The managing director (*amministratore delegato*) is responsible for company operations, with department heads

(*direttori*) reporting to him or her. Italy is a
country where decisions are made at the top. You
need to speak to a director or the president to get
your business done, and finding the right
decision-maker in a large organization with many
branches can be difficult and time-consuming.
Coporate flow charts and directories are mostly
for show and do not necessarily reflect true
responsibilities or even reporting lines.

True hierarchies are based on networks of
people who have built up personal alliances across
the organization. Different departments will have
different management styles, depending on the
boss. The primary attributes of a manager are
flexibility and pragmatism. This means that
Italian managers will focus on getting the
essentials done without overreliance on protocol,
rules, and procedures, which may be ignored.

COMPANY FINANCE AND CORPORATE GOVERNANCE

Banking investment in start-ups tends to be
minimal, and key investment funding
generally comes from other sources.
Banks cannot own commercial
companies. Those providing short-term
financing or bank product sales cannot make
medium-term loans. These are the domain of

specialized medium- and long-term credit institutions. Apart from the Banca d'Italia, which is the national regulatory bank, there are several nationwide banks with branches across the country, as well as many local banks specific to a town or region. Italy boasts the highest personal savings rate in Europe.

In the country that created accountancy in the fifteenth century, auditors tend to prepare reports that do not always correspond to the book value of the company. In due diligence proceedings, an independent auditor is advisable.

LABOR RELATIONS

Italian businesspeople work long and flexible working hours when under pressure. Executives arrive early and often stay late.

Any company in Italy with more than fifteen employees has a works committee (*consiglio di fabbrica*), with the right to monitor investment plans and working conditions.

An estimated 40 percent of the workforce is unionized, along political rather than craft lines. The main unions are Christian Democrat, Communist, and Social Democrat—known respectively as CISL, CGIL, and UIL—but there are smaller unions and workers' councils that are responsible for a large number of strikes in the public sector. It has been estimated that 25 percent of the Italian labor market is unregulated.

PLANNING
Italian companies thrive on opportunity and risk, not on planning. They will identify and exploit a niche without long-term analysis. This means that long-term joint-venture agreements will be difficult to achieve. There is a bias against long-term strategy. Italians look for short-term consistent profit.

LEADERSHIP
In most countries a key criterion for leadership is the ability to make decisions. In Italy, the key criterion is power, expressed as *autorità* (authority), *autorevolezza* (authoritativeness), and *autoritarismo* (authoritarianism). Impersonal organizational mechanisms have low validity. This means that authority resides in whomever the boss trusts. Irrespective of whether a manager is technically qualified, he or she *is* someone the boss can work with.

The Role of the Boss
"He is the boss, I am his slave," was the view of one Italian associate of the senior partner in a

Milan law firm. As befits an economy in which the family-run firm is the basic model, the management style is both authoritative and authoritarian. Decisions are made by senior people and passed down for implementation.

Although the boss (or bosses) have sole responsibility for policies and decisions, they are expected to take a human interest in their staff. They should also be *simpatico*, charismatic, and creative, and to cut a *bella figura*, while being consistent and reliable.

Italian bosses are expected to lead and to exact deference. Employees give loyalty not just because it is in their contract, but because they personally support the boss. In general, employees are suspicious of authority, and will challenge any way of working with which they do not agree.

An important part of leadership in Italy is implementation and control. Instructions and procedures are not enough. You need to get a consensus and obtain agreement. Persuasion, insistence, and follow-up are essential. This will yield flair, creativity, and hard work. But it requires intense personal input.

The first thing to do when dealing with an Italian company is to study the leadership structure, bearing in mind that the formal system may not reflect the true situation regarding power and decision making. Power may be operated by clans based on family, marriage, or wealth. The best way to find out who is important is to be prepared to mix, to socialize, and at all times to display your human side. Doing favors for people, being charming, and staying flexible are vital.

Stiffness, coldness, and bureaucracy do not go down well. Neither does doing everything by the book. The recognition that everyone has their little foibles means that an Italian manager will avoid speaking sharply or delivering moral lectures. Although there may be pressure to focus on core business, recognizing that everybody has fingers in different pies means that being involved in peripheral business may lead to greater things.

As a boss, it is important to tread a careful line between being sympathetic and accessible, and getting too close to your staff. A boss will delegate to trusted individuals, but not in terms of formal goals. Appraisals and job descriptions are rarely implemented. The key indicators monitored are cash flow, turnover, and gross profit.

The Role of the Manager
A manager's job is to display charisma to obtain a personal commitment from the workforce to the project at hand, and the drive and technical competence to implement it. Without this the

project will fail. Procedures and action plans alone will achieve little.

Multinational companies with internationally trained managers conduct business according to international procedures. In family businesses, particularly in Tuscany and Emilia-Romagna, which are run by fathers and sons and daughters, negotiation will be on a much more personal basis. The hierarchies are built less on clear responsibilities and reporting lines and more on personal alliances. Italian managers will routinely ignore procedure and rules, putting their confidence in the competence and reliability of the people they have chosen to work with, and in close personal supervision of the task.

Strategic planning is rare in Italian companies. Directors know where they want to go and broadly how to get there. If there is a plan it is not made public. The key ability of Italian managers is to spot opportunities and go for them.

The implications of this strategy for joint venture planning are obvious. Deep-rooted personal confidence is necessary to a successful business relationship, which will last only so long as it is profitable. This is what the networking and close personal contact are designed to achieve. Managers from non-Italian companies need to learn to live with it and to enjoy the ride.

DECISION-MAKING

In such a personalized management system it is obvious that delegation by department or by designated subordinate is unlikely. Delegation is to trusted individuals, wherever they are in the organization. Feedback and appraisal will be personal. That is the only environment in which personal criticism is accepted. Formal appraisals can be difficult to conduct in an Italian company. Achievement of objectives will be judged by contribution to turnover, cash flow, and profits.

The Italians feel they are good at making intuitive decisions and will back up their instincts by consulting widely. Initial decisions are often taken quite quickly but are then subjected to discussion and may change. Personal connections and personal feelings will always be part of the decision-making process.

Foreign managers should know that basing decisions purely on the figures and the business plan, or regarding decisions as "black and white" is not the Italian way. A multiplicity of factors, political, economic, and personal, come into play.

TEAMWORKING

Teams operate on the same principle as the decision-making process—top down in a family-type structure. Words like family, mutual obligation, and mutual dependence are actually used in describing team members. Teams are made up of specialists under a team leader, selected on the basis of seniority and experience, who must enjoy the personal respect of the group.

Hierarchies are respected within teams and it can be difficult for a new young team leader to make his or her presence felt. Once again, the

 family model comes to the rescue. The elder team members become "godfathers" to the young team leader and offer advice on procedure. If that does not happen, and the team's commitment is not achieved, then the opposite can occur. Older or more senior colleagues will do everything they can to undermine the younger team leader, using procedural and other devices. In this case, the only solution is to pay off and release the troublemakers.

The pace of teamwork tends to be steady and teams are happy to work together, with frequent meetings and interaction. Hours are not fixed and activities are not over-structured as this would reduce motivation. The onus is on each team member to maintain good relationships with colleagues. Showing enthusiasm for the work, and being sensitive in one's dealings with others, is important. So are socializing with other team members, remaining good-humored, and developing a positive attitude. Loyalty is a high priority. Teams may welcome support in planning and in progress chasing. Although deadlines are regarded as fixed, slippage may occur.

MOTIVATION

Enough has been said to suggest that good social relations are of above average importance for a team motivator, especially in the South. Team loyalty and appeals to the emotions are common. If, as a manager, you can provide a goal that contributes to the success of the group while helping individuals achieve their own personal goals, you will have succeeded.

THE OVERALL LANGUAGE OF MANAGEMENT

Fluency of expression is very important in Italian management. Managers will normally be good talkers. Although authoritarian in style, the tone is usually friendly and can be quite indirect, and foreigners can easily misinterpret the subtlety with which statements are made. Italians themselves frequently find the language of their British and American counterparts to be crude and overly direct by comparison.

FEEDBACK AND MANAGING DISAGREEMENT

Italians are not on the whole confrontational, but may well hit back with everything they've got if criticized directly. They are especially sensitive to accusations of volatility or disorganization.

Feedback may be given in writing in the North, but is much more likely to be oral in the South. A key feature of giving and receiving feedback is to be able to ask about and express personal feelings. So a face-to-face meeting is important in the case of disagreement. The Italians believe that any difficulty can be resolved as long as there is goodwill. Italian managers will ask you to help them on a personal basis, will show an eagerness to find solutions, and will provide you with most of the information you require. Flexibility and openness to other people's feelings are important.

COMMUNICATION STYLES

The Italians are adept at exchanging verbal information. They are less good at writing or reading memos, e-mails, and documents. In communicating with an Italian counterpart, you are far better off telephoning than writing. Many executives even telephone to say that they will be writing or that they have written. On the whole, written communication should not be allowed to stand on its own; it needs verbal backup. The further south you go in Italy, the truer this is.

Italians are also speechifiers, long on rhetoric and ideas but often short on facts. They can also be very assertive and direct and this can be seen as abrupt or dismissive. Where an Italian is at his or her most polite is in saying "No." It is important to keep the door open for other possibilities.

Good speaking skills are important and body language is used to emphasize one's point. The Italians can use intense, emotive language and be quite imaginative in their way of expressing themselves. Words like "definitely," "fantastic," and "absolutely" will be used frequently to emphasize a positive point of view.

Conversational overlap, or "ping pong" conversation, is frequent and the volume may be quite loud. Talking about yourself, your family, and your success, and revealing your emotions is accepted as a way of building good relations. Lively argument and debate are appreciated. Italians may criticize their own company in front of others and make jokes about intentions or proposals. Open disagreement and agreement is common, although it is usually done politely. Dissent is rarely final. There is always a way of resolving difficulties. Italians apologize frequently, even for small things. It is seen as part of courtesy.

Revealing oneself as human is the key to

successful face-to-face communication with
Italians in a business situation. Being responsive,
smiling, and showing interest is important.
Helping people with their problems, and telling
them your own once you have established a
relationship, is valued. So is making eye contact
and adopting a confiding tone. Ask questions to
maintain attention levels, and note any personal
information. Aim to get close to people in private.

The Italians often find the British and the
Americans cold and distant. Use relaxed body
language and try to smile. Establishing a personal
relationship will be more appreciated than a focus
on economic advantage and profit. Don't be
overassertive, overfrank, and too direct, as this
may be considered uncultured. Avoid giving too
detailed instructions and boasting, although being
confident and positive is important. It is also
important to avoid criticizing Italy—Italians may
be critical of their country, but you shouldn't be.

MAKING CONTACT

The Italians prefer to deal with people they know.
They are more open than, say, the French to "cold
contact," but they need to feel that a new contact
is *raccomandato*, i.e. recommended by a known or
recognized office or individual. This may be a
client, a chamber of commerce, or an embassy, or

personal contact through a trade fair. The initial contact may be by means of a formal letter, but this will need to be followed up by telephone calls and a personal visit. Even if you write to an Italian firm in English, small- and medium-sized companies will often reply in Italian. You may need the services of a translation agency as commercial and bureaucratic Italian has its own terminology. To avoid unnecessary delay, it is better to write your first letter in Italian.

Italian bosses, particularly in family-run firms, may not speak a foreign language, and the English-speaker in the company may be fairly low down in the chain. A senior Italian negotiator will often bring an interpreter, usually an assistant, who speaks English reasonably fluently. If so, remember to direct your conversation to your Italian counterpart, not to the assistant.

Remember that holidays are important in Italy, and that from mid-July to the end of August everything slows down. Although Italy has fewer public holidays than many Latin countries, every city celebrates its own patron saint and has its own local festival, when things close down.

BUSINESS HOURS
There is a difference between the North and the South. Northern business hours are 8:30 a.m.

until 12:45 p.m., and 3:00 p.m.
to 6 or 6:30 p.m., Monday to
Friday. In central and Southern
Italy, because of the heat, business
hours are 8:30 a.m. to 12:45 p.m.,
and 4:30 or 5:00 p.m. to 7:30 or
8:00 p.m. Many businesses are open
on Saturday morning from 8:30
to 12:45 p.m. Many Italians live
within easy commuting distance of where they
work, and go home for lunch.

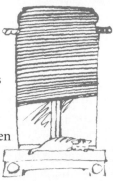

PREPARING FOR YOUR VISIT

Business has a strong social and presentational
aspect in Italy. Making a *bella figura* is important.
Ensure the clothes you take are conservative but
stylish, and that your shoes are of good quality. To
Italians, smart clothes are indicative of business
success and even casual clothes are fashionable
and chic. Trousers are fine for women, but once
again should be well-cut and stylish. Make sure
your briefcase and watch are smart. A good
ballpoint will be noticed, a scruffy ballpoint even
more! Take some family photos as well as the
business documents you need. Make sure the
documents are in tidy folders. This is all part of
creating the right stylish impression.

Italian business cards are usually printed in

plain black on a white background; as a rule, the less information they give, the more important the person.

Gift Giving

It is quite common to give a small present to any staff member who has been particularly helpful, so think about taking some modest corporate gifts—travel alarm clocks, pens, silver key fobs, diaries, or calculators. (Make sure they are name brands, but be careful that this is not seen as a crass way of highlighting your company logo.)

Any "company" gift you receive is likely to be elegant and discreet. Some Italian companies have privately published, top-quality coffee-table books and products. It is very important not to turn these down, no matter how heavy or inconvenient they may be to carry home!

THE FIRST MEETING

Small talk is important for Italians. People will want to ask you about your family and your background. This is partly a discreet way of establishing roots and confirming that you have a stake in making the business work because you have your own social responsibilities.

If you arrive in the evening and your hosts are meeting you, they may invite you for a meal. No matter how tired you are, you should accept. It will be enjoyable and relaxing, and to refuse will cause offense, and start your negotiations off on the wrong footing.

Don't be informal. The Italians are quite formal in the office and may address people by titles such as *Dottore* or *Dottoressa* for a professor or doctor, and even *Avvocato* (lawyer) or *Ingegnere* (engineer). Male and female endings are used, so the feminine of *Avoccato* is *Avvocata*, and of *Ingegnere* is *Ingegnera*, etc. The Italians also prefer to use surnames in the office, so that the person who calls one Charles at home may call one Smith in the office. In societies like Britain and North America, which tend to see the use of surnames as distancing, this form of address, often without the Mr. or Mrs., can feel quite rude. In fact, it is just a misplaced translation of an Italian practice. Younger international managers slip quite easily into first names.

As the guest, you will normally be introduced first, and the senior or eldest person present will be shown deference. Shake hands with everyone in the room on arriving, and again on leaving.

Your first meeting may not go into too much detail. Your Italian opposite number will be interested in your company and in your personal background and will tell you about his or hers. As we have seen, Italy is all about relationship-building, and this stage may be followed by lunch or at least a *panino* (bread-roll snack).

In the South it is important to allow more time for business visits. You will do twice as much in Milan as you will do in the same time in Rome or Naples. In Milan allow for, say, three meetings a day and an evening engagement. In Rome, allow for two meetings and an evening engagement and in Naples or Palermo, depending on who you are visiting, allow for two meetings in the day. Breakfast meetings have not yet caught on in Italy.

MAKING A PRESENTATION

In Italy a lecture or formal presentation should last about thirty minutes, with time for questions and discussion afterward. Audiences expect to be persuaded and appreciate a moderate to hard sell of ideas and products. The success of the presentation depends largely on the skills of the speaker, and good-quality materials matter. Formal language should be used to begin with, but informal language can also be used later. Visual aids such as films or photographs are appreciated, and should be aesthetically pleasing as well as informative. Strong eye contact is necessary, and your pace should be brisk.

Italian listeners are interested in the personality

and style of the speaker. Standing stock-still during a presentation is less appreciated than the use of body language. People may interrupt your speech for clarification, but save questions and comments for the end.

When presenting your company and your product, find out what your audience is interested in, listen for any personal details, and incorporate these into your presentation. Show an interest in them and they will reciprocate.

MEETINGS AND NEGOTIATING SKILLS

The main object of most meetings is either to communicate decisions or to discuss matters and examine issues. Some discussions may be aimed at achieving good personal relations in the interest of a long-term partnership. The Italians look for long-term profit rather than short-term gain. Meetings will often begin with a few minutes of small talk (in the South these preliminaries may last anything from twenty to thirty minutes).

Meetings rarely have a formal structure. The idea is that everyone should have the opportunity to express their point of view. People may all talk at once, or even conduct mini-conversations or take telephone calls in the room. This is not considered rude. Work around it; don't get upset.

Even if there is an agenda, it is not considered

necessary to take each point in order and people happily return to items raised previously. Agendas, action points, time frames, next steps, and even minutes are not considered seriously in most Italian companies, as the decision will be made by people who may not even be present.

Negotiations can be finalized quite quickly, but Italian negotiators are also very patient, can go into great detail, and may take time to achieve their aims. Their approach can be quite subtle. The Italians like win-win outcomes, and may take a piece of secondary business if they cannot get the main contract they were after. Establishing a contractual relationship is the way to a longer and more fulfilling relationship.

The Italians may move quickly to apparent agreement but then take quite a long time to discuss the details, which may substantially change the nature of the contract. Discussion, though intense, is conducted in a pleasant way and Italians can be very accommodating, especially if personal considerations are involved.

A word of caution: while it is important to express optimism and not to knock your negotiating partner's enthusiasm, try to separate facts from speculation and check that your Italian counterparts are not promising more than they can deliver. A good way to do this is to take notes that you can check later. It may also be useful to periodically summarize what has been agreed to.

Always listen carefully to advice from your Italian partners and respect their know-how. They understand Italy much better than you do and they are also very experienced in world markets.

BUSINESS ENTERTAINING
The Italians like to get to know their partners, and this takes place over long and leisurely meals. On the whole, they do not like to conclude business without lunch, dinner, or at least a *panino* to "set the seal" on the relationship, and they are very good at choosing the right restaurant, food, and wine. Entertaining is usually semiformal, or formal, in a good restaurant with excellent wine and food. Dress is either smart or casual, but always elegant, with matching accessories. The conversation may be about business in general, but will very often turn to art, history, or regional culture. Avoid topics such as the Second World War, politics, corruption, and the Mafia. It is normal to keep your hands on the table when not eating, and you should be on your best and most charming behavior.

Remember that when meeting for the first time in a business setting, people will introduce themselves by their surname, not by their company or their job, which would be considered gauche or even rude. Do not go to first names until you are invited to do so. On the whole, guests leave when they are ready; it is considered rude for the host to end the meal. In the South, the host often arranges transport home for guests.

If going to someone's home, the same rules apply. You are expected to bring a gift (perhaps flowers, or gift-wrapped chocolates), but be careful about giving wine unless it is of high quality, as many Italians are connoisseurs and may even have their own vineyards. Liqueurs, delicacies, and craft items from your own country are all suitable gifts; whiskeys and liqueurs are usually appreciated.

The Italian genius for entertaining can pose a problem if you are returning the favor. If you are inviting a business acquaintance while you are in Italy, it is a good idea to ask his or her secretary to recommend a favorite restaurant, and to defer to your guest in the choice of food and wine. This will be taken as a compliment.

Even if you are entertaining in your own country, you will find that most Italians prefer eating Italian food, so look for the most authentic Italian restaurant available. Your guest may also know of a wonderful restaurant (perhaps owned by a relative) that you have never heard of but that serves food to die for. All you need do is pay the bill.

chapter nine

COMMUNICATING

LANGUAGE SKILLS

Italy is a country of communicators, but not always
successfully in English. Although English is taught
in primary school, many Italians (especially the
older generation) are not particularly confident
English-speakers. For those who are, their English is
often quite heavily accented, with the vowels strung
out musically, extending the length of words and
sentences. It is important not to expect everyone to
understand English. There are two ways of dealing
with this: one is to make allowances with your
English, and the other is to learn some Italian. Both
approaches should be adopted.

Using English

Speaking English clearly isn't a matter of slowing
down, it's a matter of leaving pauses so that your
interlocutor can catch up. So speak a little more
slowly and clearly than you would normally, but
leave a short gap (a mere beat will do) between
sentences or phrases to allow the conversation
to breathe.

Secondly, avoid idioms and slang. And if you use initials or acronyms, spell them out the first time you use them as they will probably be different in Italian.

Finally, it's clearer if you use shorter sentences and make them active ("I do it") rather than passive ("it is done") if possible.

Learn Some Italian

Many universities and private language schools in Italy offer short courses in Italian for foreigners from two weeks' to three months' duration. Courses cover both Italian language and culture, ranging from Etruscan history to contemporary Italian literature and art. Florence has some twenty-five foreign language schools teaching Italian, and there are two state-funded organizations, the *Università Italiana per Stranieri* in Perugia, and the *Scuola Lingue e Cultura per Stranieri* in Siena. Study grants may be available and it is worth inquiring at the Italian Consulate or Italian Cultural Institute. Perugia and Siena run courses year-round, as do private language schools. Universities usually only offer courses during the summer vacation.

THE MEDIA
Newspapers and Magazines
Italians aren't such avid newspaper readers as the

British or the North Americans, and readership
is greater in the North than in the South.
Newspapers are published regionally, but some
have national circulation. All newspapers have
political leanings and it is useful to know
about these.

Italy's best-selling newspapers are *Repubblica*,
published in Rome and holding center-left
views; the Milan-based *Corriere della Sera*,
which holds center-right views and includes
an English section; and *Italy Daily*, which is
more centrist. *L'Unità*, Italy's Communist
newspaper, is also influential although less
widely read. A number of regional
newspapers are also important, such as *La
Nazione* (Florence), *La Stampa* (Turin), *Il
Tempo* and *Il Messaggero* (Rome), *Il Secolo
X1X* (Genoa), and *La Sicilia* (Catania). The
main Italian news magazine is *L'Espresso*.

Italy doesn't have downscale tabloid newspapers,
but the specialist sports papers *Corriere dello Sport*
and *La Gazzetta dello Sport* have a wide
readership. Gossip magazines like *Oggi* (Today)
and *Gente* (People) are very popular. This is where
you'll find the paparazzi pictures.

Several English-language magazines are available in the big cities. You can ask for *Time Out Rome* (monthly), *Where Rome* (monthly), or *A Guest in Milan* (monthly) at your hotel, though they usually run out early in the day.

Newsdealers are uncommon in Italy. Instead there are state-run kiosks (*edicole*) all over the cities. They are where Italians buy the popular weekly part-work magazines with CD-Roms or videos on any number of subjects.

The international press is well represented in Italy. The *New York Herald Tribune* is one of the most popular papers. The weekly news magazine *The Economist* is also widely read.

Radio and TV
Italian radio has an audience of 35 million people. Since deregulation in 1976, the number of stations has grown to around two and a half thousand. The state radio, Rai, runs three stations, two of which have pop and light music, while the other (Radio 3) broadcasts discussion programs and classical music. For Italian and international music on commercial stations, try Radio Italia, Radio Globo, or Radio DJ.

For English-language radio, the BBC World Service broadcasts to Italy. For a program guide, contact BBC World Service Publicity at PO Box 46, Bush House, London WC2B 4PH.

A magazine *On Air* is also available at
onairmagazine@bbc.co.uk. If you have access to
satellite TV in Italy, you can receive BBC 1, 2, 3,
and 4, and also Radio Canada, Radio Australia,
and Voice of America. To access BBC programs
online, go to www.bbc.co.uk.

Television

After the Portuguese and the British, Italians
watch more TV than any other European nation
(on average, about four hours per day). Surveys
suggest that 90 percent of Italians watch some TV
every day and that most receive their news from
TV. There is little or no cable TV in Italy, but wide
use of satellite TV (see below) from the Astra
satellite. Imported programs are dubbed into
Italian. Violent or sexually explicit programs cannot
be shown between 7:00 a.m. and 10:30 p.m.—it
was the Italians who pioneered the "violence chip"
that filters out violent programs when children
are watching.

Until 1976 all TV was state-owned and
censored by the Church. Since deregulation,
however, Italy has acquired six main stations and
hundreds of local ones. Of the six main terrestrial
stations, three are run by the state: Rai 1, Rai 2,
and Rai 3. The state channels command about
half of the regular viewing audience.

The main commercial stations—Italia 1, Rete 4,

and Canale 5—are owned by Silvio Berlusconi through his Mediaset company and command about 50 percent of the viewing audience.

The remaining 10 percent of the audience watch programs put out by the approximately nine hundred local TV stations.

Italian TV is not noted for the quality of its programing. The key issue, however, is that in a country where TV is the main opinion-former, the entire private sector is owned by one person, who is also the leader of a political party.

Satellite TV
Pay TV is very popular in Italy, with over a million subscribers. The advantage of pay TV and satellite TV is that they offer much wider access to English-language programs. The *doppio* audio track allows you to bring up the original English-language soundtrack. You can also receive BBC World TV and other English-language stations such as CNN.

TV Systems
Standard PAL, NTSC, and SECAM videos won't work in Italy, which uses the PAL-BG system. It's best not to import a TV or video into Italy, but to buy a multi-standard system locally. Italy is a Zone 2 DVD area, so U.S. Zone 1 DVDs can only be viewed on a multi-standard DVD player.

TELEPHONES

The Italian state telephone company is Telecom Italia but, like Britain and the U.S.A., other suppliers are now in the market, notably Tiscali and Wind. All major towns have a Telecom Italia office, which is responsible for the installation and maintenance of phone lines. Telecom Italia is the first port of call if you are getting a new phone line installed or changing the subscriber name, but the phone itself may be provided by another company.

Dialing Codes

In most countries area codes begin with a (0), and when you dial from abroad you omit the zero. In Italy you don't. So if you are dialing a number in Florence, for example, which is 00 39 (0)55…, you should dial 00 39 055 followed by the subscriber number. If you forget, a recorded message will remind you, but in Italian only. All calls, even local ones within the area you are calling from, require the area code to be entered. Dialing out is much simpler: simply 00 and the country code.

Many Italians now have mobile phones. To call someone on their mobile, you must always dial the area code before the number, even if you are in the area.

Answering the Phone

Italian has a universal greeting for answering the phone: "*Pronto.*" If you hear an answering machine message, it will probably be something like "We are momentarily absent." No Italian will let you know that they have gone away for three weeks as it would be considered tantamount to an invitation to burglars.

Using Public Telephones

This can be tricky as public pay phones are frequently out of order. You will need to buy a phone card (*carta/scheda/tessera telefonica*) from a *tabacchi* (tear off the marked corner first).

If you need a landline, go to one of the numerous telephone centers that have sprung up in the cities. In the countryside, bars or restaurants may still have a *telefono a scatti* (points telephone), which records the number of units of each call. The barman switches on the phone for you and you pay him for the units used.

In the countryside, some houses display a telephone symbol that means they are authorized as public phone-service providers.

Finding a Phone Number

Telecom Italia publishes directories in two formats, *Pagine Bianche* (White Pages) for personal numbers, and *Pagine Gialle* (Yellow

Pages) for business. You can also access them on the Internet at www.paginegialle.it and www.paginebianche.it.

An English Yellow Pages service is available for major cities at www.englishyellowpages.it. Directory inquiries in Italy are accessed by dialing 12, but the procedure is automated and you have to hold for a human voice. There is no English directory inquiries service.

Emergencies

Italy's general emergency number is 113. Local operators speak only Italian but a translation service into English is available on 170.

THE POSTAL SERVICE

The PT (*Poste e Telecomunicazioni*) is a limited company with a 75 percent government holding. Traditionally, the postal service in Italy is considered extremely unreliable and most Italians prefer to use registered post (*posta raccomandata*) or a private courier service for anything important. The most reliable postal service is from the Vatican in Rome, which sends all its international mail from Switzerland, so you get interesting Vatican stamps and safe delivery too! All the major courier services have offices in the main cities. U.S. Mailboxes Inc. now has several franchisees in Italy.

Italy has an ordinary postal service (*posta ordinaria*) and a priority service (*posta prioritaria*). *Posta prioritaria* guarantees delivery within Italy on the next working-day, and in three to four days within the EU. You need a gold priority stamp and an airmail sticker for foreign destinations. There's also a *Postacelere* express service available in main post offices. For anything important make sure you obtain proof of posting.

Postcards and letters (if they arrive) will take three to seven days within Italy, and four to ten days within Europe. Allow at least a week for airmail letters to North America; for Australia and New Zealand, two weeks.

The best place to buy stamps is in a *tabacchi* (marked with a black T sign). Stamps (*francobolli*) are sold loose, not in booklets. The official identification color of the post office is red, although documentation is often done in blue. There is usually only one collection per day.

Post offices get very busy and have different windows for different services, so make sure you are in the right line. Post offices deal with telegrams, faxes, telex, foreign currency exchange, cash transfers, utility bills, road tax, and TV licenses. You can buy the *bollo* for the car in the post office. They also pay state pensions and deal in lottery tickets. Unless your business specifically needs a post office or you have plenty of time, you are better off buying stamps in a *tabacchi* and posting in a mailbox. Main post offices are open all day during the week but close at 1:00 p.m. on Saturdays.

Sending Mail to Italy
Italian addresses have a five-digit postcode, or CAP (*codice di avviamento postale*). It is important to get this right to ensure delivery. You can find postcode details at www.poste.it. Here is the normal way of writing an Italian address:

> Maggiore Paolo
> (surname followed by first name)
> Via Marghera, 2
> I-10234 Torino
> Italy

CONVERSAZIONE
So far, we've looked at electronic communication, but the communication that really matters to Italians is face-to-face. *Conversazione* originally meant associating with others, and it is here that the Italians excel. They will go to great lengths to draw you in to conversation, and every town has its piazza, which is essentially a space for conversation. *Stare insieme* (being together) is important for Italians as it gives a chance to air grievances, express feelings, and defuse flare-ups.

Even on the beach, where the British and the Americans will walk miles to find a lonely cove, the Italians will crowd deck chair to deck chair in a good-neighborly fashion.

A new venue for *conversazione* is provided by the TV talk shows, which are exceptionally popular and go on for hours.

Body Language

An amusing way of passing time is to sit in a café and watch Italians talking. They talk with their hands, and their gestures can be very expressive, particularly in Naples and the South. A person who is expressing disagreement may stroke their fingers upward under their chin, palm down, and then thrust them forward. At a football match, you may see people pointing their hands at the referee with the "pinky" and forefinger out and the other fingers and thumb turned in, palm down. This means that the spectators disagree with the referee. If the palm is turned upward in the same gesture, then you know that they are saying something obscene to the referee.

Greetings and Forms of Address

Despite its charm and openness, Italy is quite a formal society. Italian has the formal "you" (*Lei*) and the informal "you" (*tu*). You should remain on formal terms until invited to use first names, though this doesn't apply when you are with children, teenagers, or young adults, or in an informal environment. As a guest you will always be introduced first.

Shaking hands is a physical affair. Hands will be shaken warmly and your arm may be grasped with the other hand. Friends and male relatives will often embrace or slap each other on the back in greeting, and women (and sometimes men) will kiss on both cheeks. At a large gathering, it is considered acceptable to go up to someone, shake hands, and introduce yourself.

Topics of Conversation

Most Italians are highly cultured people, and will be happy to talk about art, architecture, and monuments, particularly in their local area. Local food and wine are popular subjects, and sports are very important. Don't treat soccer lightly—it is taken seriously by many Italians. Family, local scenery, holidays, and movies are other favorite topics of conversation.

As mentioned previously, although Italians are often critical of things in their country, they do not appreciate it when foreigners criticize them. Religion, politics, and the Second World War are off-limits, and sexually explicit jokes are not usually exchanged in mixed company.

GENDER ISSUES

The downside of "romantic Italy" has always been the impression that foreign women are "fair game." In fact, Italian women are on the whole strictly brought up, and Italian men live at home longer than their counterparts in the U.S. or U.K. In the North, it is acceptable (though still unusual) for a single woman to eat alone in a restaurant. In the South, however, people are less accustomed to this idea, and you may attract unwanted attention. One way to show that you do not wish to be bothered is to keep work or reading matter on your table.

CONCLUSION

Italy, as we have seen, is a land of contradictions, combining conformity and anarchy, bureaucracy and evasion, extreme riches and great poverty, scandal and religion. One writer has compared Italy's shining surface with its "dark heart."

And yet what keeps Italy and the Italians going is the conviction that the one loyalty that matters is family and close friends, and that with time and understanding everything can be worked out. It is only a matter of finding the way. This fluidity makes life in Italy exceptionally attractive, even seductive, for foreigners, although for residents and business people it can be frustrating.

Modern Italy faces unemployment, immigration (particularly from the Balkans), environmental pollution, rising housing costs and crime, and the social fallout from economic reform. However, it has overcome political extremism and achieved a degree of government stability, and is one of the main upholders and beneficiaries of the EU and the euro.

Italy has one of the largest economies in the world, and is a powerhouse of manufacturing ingenuity and creativity in food, fashion design, and the automotive industry. The Italians are a vital, warmhearted, and inventive people whose contribution to Western civilization cannot be overestimated, and who have contributed hugely to the gaiety of nations.

Further Reading

History, Politics, and Society

Barzini, Luigi. *The Italians*. London: Penguin Books, 1983.

Ginsborg, Paul. *Italy and its Discontents*. London: Penguin Books, 2003.

Jones, Tobias. *The Dark Heart of Italy*. London: Faber and Faber, 2003.

Keates, Jonathan. *The Rough Guide: History of Italy*. London: Penguin Books, 2003.

Lintner, Valerio. *A Traveller's History of Italy*. London: Windrush Press/Cassell, 2001.

Richards, Charles. *The New Italians*. London: Penguin Books, 1994.

Guides

Belford, Ros, *et al.The Rough Guide to Italy*. London: Rough Guides, 2003.

Simonis, D., and F. Adams, M. Roddis, S. Webb, and N. Williams. *Lonely Planet Italy*. London: Lonely Planet, 2003.

Streiffert, Anna. *Eyewitness Guide to Italy*. London: Dorling Kindersley, 2003.

Living in Italy

Chesters, Graeme (ed). *Living and Working in Italy*. London: Survival Books, 2003.

Flower, Raymond, and Alessandro Falassi. *Culture Shock! Italy*. Portland, Oregon: Graphic Arts Center Publishing, 1995/London: Kuperard, 2003.

Hinton, Amanda. *Living and Working in Italy*. Oxford: How To Books, 2003.

Morrison, Terri, and Wayne A. Conaway and George A. Borden. *Kiss, Bow, or Shake Hands: How to Do Business in Sixty Countries*. Avon, Massachusetts: Adams Media Corporation, 1994.

Parks, Tim. *An Italian Education*. London: Vintage Books, 2000.

——. *Italian Neighbours*. London: Vintage Books, 2001.

——. *A Season with Verona*. London: Vintage Books, 2003.

Index

Acknowledgments

The author would like to acknowledge the contributions of Hugh Shankland, Professor of Italian at the University of Durham, and the work of Barry Tomalin, Chief Consultant of CultureShock! Consulting, in the preparation of this book.